D1830046

Tropical Ecstasy

Tropical Ecstasy

A nostalgia trip back to Brazil after an absence of twenty-five years

with a gazetteer and glossary of local lingo

by Norman Weeks

N.W.

Norman Weeks

Tropical Ecstasy

ISBN: 979-8-6052-1359-8

Copyright © 2020 by Norman Weeks

Norman Weeks, publisher. Published through Kindle Direct Publishing.

Tropical Ecstasy is also available as an eBook at amazon.com

To the people of Penedo, Alagoas, Brazil

Tropical Ecstasy

Preface: *Saudades* and Reminiscences 7

Amazônia and Manaus 17

Recife and Olinda, Pernambuco 75

Maceió, Alagoas 118

***Destino*: Penedo, Alagoas** 153

Return 255

Gazetteer 268

Glossary 275

Preface: *Saudades* and Reminiscences

«*Um vagabundo como eu não merece ser feliz....*» The words of an old Brazilian pop tune. ('A bum like me doesn't deserve to be happy.')

'...Doesn't deserve to be happy.' Yet, somehow or other, I have succeeded in becoming happy, without any merit on my part. It was love that brought happiness. It's better to be lucky than worthy.

A happy man, why, then, don't I stay home with the one who has made me happy? Because I'm still a *vagabundo.*

When I went to obtain my visa, the clerk in the consulate in Chicago asked me in Portuguese, «*Vai matar as saudades do Brasil, hem?*» , ('Going to kill your *saudades* of Brazil, eh?') «*Sim,*» ('Yes'), I answered.

I'm going back to Brazil because of *saudades.* That very Brazilian word and its various deepfelt meanings! What are *saudades?* Homesickness? No, there's no home for me in Brazil. Nostalgia? Yes, nostalgia for my life as it was twenty-five years ago. Longing? Certainly, I'm going to satisfy my longing. I miss Brazil. That's why I'm going back.

But *matar* means to kill. Is that what you have to do to *saudades,* kill them, kill them off? I don't want to kill my *saudades,* I want to embrace them. *Um abraço* (a warm embrace) of all my *saudades!* I am returning to Brazil, not to kill anything off, but to throw loving arms around my past.

A month in Brazil. First, Amazônia, a new experience. Then, *a minha viagem de saudades* (my nostalgia trip), to the *nordeste,* the Northeast region, and some of its vividly remembered places:—Recife and Olinda, Maceió, and my ultimate destination, *o nosso querido Penedo* (our dear Penedo).

In Portuguese, destination and destiny are expressed by the same word. I am going to my *destino.*

* * * * *

When speakers of our English find out that I speak Portuguese, they usually say to me, "Oh, that's a difficult language, isn't it?"

Not really.

Portuguese is one of the five plebian granddaughters of that grand aristocratic lady, classical Latin. The descendants have little of the sophistication of their granny. The passage of linguistic generations has been a vulgarization and consequent simplification; none of the Romance languages presents the challenge encountered in learning Latin.

In Portuguese, the number of forms of verb conjugations—a difficult memorization task of inflected languages—is a fraction of those in Latin. Gone, too, is declension of nouns, replaced by easy prepositions and a simplified, although sometimes peculiar, singular/ plural. Portuguese does retain from Latin a gender for all nouns, that bugaboo to English speakers, unaccustomed as we are to think of sexless objects in terms of gender. Some of the romance of the Romance languages is inflected and inflicted upon the inert.

The vocabulary of Portuguese is poor compared to English, as I once verified by comparing the Portuguese and English sections of the dictionary published by the Ministry of Education and Culture of Brazil. Brazilian

Portuguese has added to European Portuguese many African and native Indian words, but its assimilation of foreign vocabulary is nothing compared to the bulging sponge of English. Because English has drawn nearly half of its own vocabulary from Latin and the Romance languages, many Portuguese words will sound familiar to you; you will be able to guess their meanings.

Some aspects of Portuguese are very easy. To ask a question, for example, one that solicits a yes-or-no answer, you merely make a statement and throw in an upward vocal inflection at the end. Like Latin, syntax in Portuguese is loose, virtually slapdash. You'll rarely be out-of-order, when you try to say something in Portuguese.

Nor is spelling any challenge. Portuguese has a close correspondence between the written language and the spoken one; what you see is what you say. Accent marks show you which syllable is to be stressed. Brazilian school children are spared the struggle with spelling that so confounds American children (and adults).

And the pronunciation? Well, it's much easier to learn new sounds when one is a small child, but, even later, we can still parrot.

No, the Portuguese language is no braincracker. That is not to say that you can learn it on a weekend.

Those who think Portuguese is a difficult language confuse the difficult with the merely unfamiliar. Yet, Portuguese should become more familiar. It is now in the top ten of spoken languages (put there not by any doings of the sardine-fishers of Portugal, but by the population explosion of Brazil; not a cultural achievement, admittedly).

Another misconception about Portuguese is that it is close to French. That notion must be due to the fact that both languages have so many nasal sounds that people take them as twins. The nasal sounds are quite different, however. As you probably know, all the French nasals are pronounced with the nose held high in the air.

Historically and structurally, Portuguese is closest to Spanish, as Portugal is geographically closest to Spain. I consider Portuguese almost a fellow dialect of Spanish; you could argue with me about what is dialect, what is distinct language. The pronunciations of Portuguese and Spanish have diverged, which makes difficult a test of affinity by verbal exchange. Yet I, who have never studied a word of Spanish, once attended an Isabel Sarli film festival, and the actors spoke their Argentine Spanish with such slow, clear cadence that, from my good grasp of Portuguese, I understood most of what I heard. (Of course, the looking helped, too.) A Spanish speaking person can read Portuguese, and vice-versa, which demonstrates the structural affinity. French is a couple of steps away.

Let's look at a common item of vocabulary in the five Romance languages. Take the word *all.* From the Latin root *totus,* in Portuguese *all* is *tudo;* in Spanish, *todo;* in French, *tout;* in Italian, *tutto;* in Romanian, *toto.*

You could almost say that the closeness of the Romance languages varies directly with geographical distance, Italian the most subject to the pull-of-gravity of the Latin of ancient Rome. If you study more than one Romance language, as I have, the similarities will present problems. You'll confuse your *tudo* with your *todo,* and a lot else besides, until you find yourself speaking *total* babel. I myself sometimes let slip a Latin, French, or Italian word into my Portuguese.

Now, I don't pretend to be a philologist or linguist. So, what's the point of this seemingly academic essay on Portuguese, when, instead, I should be packing my clothes for Brazil? Are you impatient to be off? Well, we have to pack our minds, too.

Being able to speak Portuguese in Brazil is not a mere condescension or concession to the locals. As a practical consideration, you'll need some knowledge of Portuguese to get your needs met, for you'll find few English-speakers, if, as I am about to do, you venture into rural Brazil. More importantly, before you go to Brazil, before you travel to any other culture, really, you've got to step out of your own frame-of-reference, linguistic and cultural. Let's go to Brazil? O.K. then, let's speak some Portuguese.

I'm just a vagabond polyglot who likes to have a few words with the locals as I pass through. In Brazil, those will be Portuguese words. I try to be fluent in the language of Romance.

If I proceed from linguistic analytics to personal aesthetics, I can, with more confidence of immunity from contradiction by academics, speak from experience.

I think the sound of Portuguese spoken by a young woman is the most beautiful sound made by the human voice, never mind that hefty soprano's caterwauling and that tenor's loud drone.

I once listened to two young ladies—they were daughters of the gardener of the Rio de Janeiro zoo. As I engaged them in conversation by the fountain on the shaded path, I was enchanted by the loveliest, most exquisitely charming, vocal sounds I have ever heard; (my apologies to *i signori* Verdi and Puccini).

Now, you might conjecture that my youthful romantic eroticism deobjectified my linguistic appraisal. Maybe so. Do I love Brazilian girls because they speak Portuguese, or do I love Portuguese because it is spoken by Brazilian girls? Both, I suppose. Medium and message, I don't distinguish them.

The feminine voice of Portuguese is the song of the angels. ...

* * * * *

"Normando Gives a Portuguese Lesson"

During my Peace Corps days, when I was residing on my *sítio* (rural homestead) outside Penedo, there was a boy about nine years old who lived down the road from me. João used to show up and hang around, offering to do those odd jobs I wanted to do for myself. On a Peace Corps subsistence allowance, I was in no position to be hiring a houseboy or any other domestic help.

One day, I was looking for a good fallen coconut to hack open with my machete for a morning drink. I found one.

As usual, João interposed himself to offer help. Picking up another coconut and handing it to me, he said, *«Olha, seu Normando! Isto é mais bom.»* ('Look, Norman, sir, this one is more good!')

Correcting his Portuguese, I told him, *«Não mais bom, João. Melhor.»* ('Not *more good,* Johnny. *Better.*')

To which João answered agreeably, *«Sim, seu Normando. Isto é muito mais bom melhor!»* ('Yes, Norman, sir, this one is much more good better!')

* * * * *

One day, I asked João why he wasn't in school.

I translate our conversation:

"Because I don't have clothes to wear to school."

"What clothes do you need?"

"A shirt. I don't have a good shirt. And a pair of shorts. And sandals."

"How much would a shirt, and shorts, and sandals cost?"

João told me. It didn't sound like very much.

"João, you should be in school," I said. Then I gave him the money. "Here, buy the clothes you need and go to school."

"Yes, Norman, sir," João said, taking the money and heading home.

A few days later, he showed up at my *sítio* in the middle of the morning, wearing just his usual one item of clothing, dirty, ragged, faded shorts.

"João, why aren't you in school?"

"I don't have clothes for school."

"But I gave you money to buy clothes."

"Yes, Norman, sir, but when I showed the money to my mother, she took it away from me to buy food. And that's why I'm not in school. I don't have the clothes to go to school."

* * * * *

I remember that, during our Peace Corps training, we were shown a very explicit color movie of childbirth.

The mother-to-be's agonized screams in the distress of labor made me feel faint; her expectancy was my apprehension.

I fled the room in the middle of a contraction. I wasn't used to such things; no woman had ever lain down, opened her legs, and delivered a baby on the sofa in the living room of our family apartment on Draper Street.

After a few minutes of my own deep breathing in the corridor, I regained my composure and was able to return to my box seat. The birth proving a protracted process and the film unedited, I hadn't missed much. I enjoyed the climax of the show.

I didn't feel too conspicuous about those minutes in the corridor, because I was not there alone. A few other trainees—(all male, by the way)—joined me in my swoon. Not all of them mustered the courage to go back in.

Now, why had the Peace Corps thought such a presentation necessary to our training? I knew that the population of Brazil was growing by leaps and bounds—that had been explained to us—; but might I be ambling down some dirt road one day and find another pedestrian in labor? Or might I be on a social call, when, during the middle of my chat with the family, two or three of the women of the house would lift their skirts and proceed to squeeze out babies? Or would the locals, knowing how hygienic Americans are, send their women over to my house to drop their offspring into my clean hands?

In the course of my Peace Corps work, I might be called upon to administer first aid; that apparently included the firstest of first aid. A foreigner barely arrived in the country, would I be grabbing into the innermost privates of the locals?; would *that* be the perspective from which I would be seeing Brazil?

Our group was training for a program in education, not in health or medicine. I would have thought a film of a typical rural Brazilian school in session more appropriate. My job description said ABCs, not the raw facts-of-life.

Maybe the film was meant as sobering reality to caution the males in our training group. We would be serving two years in Brazil, plenty of time to participate in both childbegetting and childbearing. We, who might be cause, should witness the consequence. Yet, are obstetricians less interested in sex than accountants are? Do butchers become vegetarians?

Whatever the reason for including that film in our training, during the two years I spent in Brazil—pregnant women all around me—I never once had the opportunity to put my childbirth training to use.

I would follow pregnant women down the street, hoping to be on-the-spot in the nick-of-time; but something would happen to prevent me from assisting. I'd drop the bowl of hot water, for example, and, by the time I'd come back from fetching another one, the woman would be carrying the baby in her arms and discussing names for it with the neighbors.

Or I'd follow one particular woman every day for months. She would get bigger and bigger and bigger, until I was dizzy with suspense. But no baby ever came out. That woman had a perpetual pregnancy.

Once, I climbed through the window of the clinic in Penedo, into the delivery room, but I was driven out as a suspected molester by a dozen outraged expectant mothers. I only wanted to help!

How I regret my failure as a Peace Corps volunteer. Despite my excellent training, I just could not deliver.

Amazônia and Manaus

Tuesday, March 14, 1995. In transit, Chicago-Miami-Manaus.

On the flight down:

All the ponds, lakes, rivers, and flooded lowlands of North America glinted in the sun like shards of a broken mirror.

My sunglasses polarized the sunlight reflected from the waters below, tracing a blinding green that proceeded with the plane...more shards of ponds, streaking iridescence of streams and rivers.

The waters beyond and nearer the green running line of my vision were pink, while those in the far distance were ice-blue, like the winter just left behind in Illinois.

My sunglasses, asserting certain hues of the spectrum, gave me a brilliant, already tropical, show. As the sun shone through the plane window, even the clear plastic drinking glass in my hand displayed a rainbow.

A polarized lens reveals the components of light more beautiful than the totality; but, after a while, my awe became eyestrain, so I pulled down the shade against the sun, which was now low in the sky and heating my body through my shirt as I sat in a window seat.

Chicago to Miami, less than three hours. Over central Florida, the Swamp, a little preview of coming attractions—Amazônia! Back in Chicago, all is still winter-brown, the last pile of snow in the neighborhood, that in the shadow of the north wall of our dining room, melted just yesterday. The robins arrived two days ago.

Florida, on the way to Brazil. Florida, with its canalized streams. Will they ever canalize the Amazon?

Then, on the flight out of the United States, I spoke my first words in Portuguese to a Brazilian on this, my nostalgia trip. And the Varig stewardess gave me a knowing smile.

The movie on the flight to Manaus was about terror on a whitewater rafting trip. What an ominous psychological preparation for my Amazon cruise. River of risks! River of danger! River of death!

Wednesday, March 15. Manaus.

International air passengers are like bats, departing at dusk, in the air all night, then, just before dawn, coming to the perch and ready for a full day's sleep.

We arrived in Manaus at 4:00 A.M. Many of the passengers were members of a senior citizens' tour group. They already looked the worse for wear. Maybe this jungle excursion was not such a good idea after all, some of them may be thinking.

The Immigration officer, a solid mass of a man, more like a marine sergeant than a paper pusher, yawned with early-morning sleepiness, as he examined and stamped the passports and checked that we had filled out identification cards that we would have to present to the police in case of any trouble in Brazil. I gave him the greetings of the day in Portuguese, and he answered with as polite a geniality as he could muster at that hour.

Baggage pickup was speedy, and my driver was waiting for me outside the terminal exit door.

It was still dark, so I couldn't get much of a first view of Manaus. My driver gave me some background on local tourism and the manufacturing economy, but I found his Portuguese difficult, a strange accent, as if Portuguese were not his first language; perhaps he speaks the Indian dialect of his childhood at home.

I asked to proceed directly to the *Amazon Clipper*, where I could get a few hours' snooze before departure; but my driver told me that the boat wouldn't arrive dockside until midday.

After the 4-1/2 hours in Miami airport, then the

long intercontinental flight, would I have to wait nodding for eight more hours in the lobby of the Hotel Tropical, until the casting-off?

I talked the situation over with the reception clerk in the Tropical. He proposed a room at half-rate for my part-day, so I checked in.

A refreshing shower, a love-note discovered hidden in my suitcase. The insomnia of excitement, a few aspirins, but some rest, anyway. Feeling OK, ready to go!

* * * * *

Aboard the *Amazon Clipper*:

She's a fine boat, proud and white, double-decked, with, on the upper deck, a covered walkway on both sides and open observation areas fore and aft.

My cabin is amidships on the upper deck, a choice location, away from the constant rumble and fumes of the diesel engine below. My room is equipped with a bunk bed, a private toilet and shower, and air conditioning that enters from a tube in the wall.

There are only seven passengers for our four-day cruise: A honeymooning couple from Barcelona, a married couple, Italians turned Canadian, a shapely Brazilian woman and her German male, and myself. Five crew members are aboard.

The young couple from Barcelona seem an awkward match. He is young in years but middle-aged in his manner, reserved, maintaining his Catalan dignity. She, by contrast, is a child, sweet and smiling in a simple way. Her name is Miranda.

The Italian couple. . . Well, I think of them as Italian, although they have been citizens of Canada for thirty years. Their English is Italianate, the only Canadianism about them their acquired habit of appending "eh?" to statements they make.

They are well traveled, but both of them have fuzzy notions about where they've been. They'll begin to tell a story, only to forget the name of the place they were going to tell me about.

I happened to mention Hawaii to the wife. She didn't like it, she said; she'd been to Acapulco once. When I told her that Acapulco was in Mexico, she was surprised and confused. Which was the one she didn't like, then?; was it Hawaii or Mexico? Well, no matter. She was somewhere else now.

When I asked her where she was originally from, she said, "Near Naples." "Oh, in Campania?", I said helpfully. "No. San Bartolomeo, Benevento, near Foggia." Now I was the one frowning in geographical confusion.

What good does travel do, anyway? We're lucky if we can appreciate where we're at, let alone where we've been or where we intend to go.

I soon understood that this jungle cruise was the husband's idea. She has come along, but mostly to read books on deck, as if the Amazon were the Atlantic and there would be long hours with nothing to look at but blue water and blue sky. Her reading tastes are UFOs and apparitions of angels, in large-print, illustrated editions.

She is deathly afraid of snakes. Amazônia is the wrong place to be for a person with that kind of phobia. Her husband ridicules her fear to the rest of us.

The husband and I got into a discussion of economics and politics in Canada and the United States. Even in the jungle, politics!

The German told me that he sells equipment to steel mills in Brazil; he comes to Brazil on business a few times a year.

He has apparently found a tropical reception in Neilde, his Brazilian *namorada* (sweetheart). She is from Vitória, the capital of the state of Espírito Santo. Neilde speaks only Portuguese; he understands it but speaks it haltingly. Despite that, they communicate well, mostly in hand-and-body language.

Neilde is latched on to him, perhaps to make the most of his transient stays in Brazil. I would find her unfriendly, for a Brazilian, but, given the situation, I can understand her narrow communicative focus.

Like many Germans, he can get along in English, so I tried to make conversation with him, a little shoptalk at least. Rummaging through the clutter of trivia in my mind, I dug up the name Volta Redonda, a steel mill in Brazil. I was going to throw out the name to further the conversation, when it occurred to me that my Brazilian steel mill knowledge was a quarter-century old. Not wanting to appear ill-informed, I asked the German only whether Volta Redonda was still operating. He told me he wasn't sure.

After a thoughtful pause, he informed me that Volta Redonda had been given to Brazil as a gift from the United States, in gratitude for Brazil's dispatchment of soldiers to Europe in the last days of World War II, yes, Volta Redonda, an American thank-you to the Brazilians for the latter's participation in the chore of killing Germans.

Oops! No lingering hard feelings, I hoped.

A bit later, the German remarked to me, "I saw you in the lobby of the Hotel Tropical before our cruise, and I said to Neilde, 'That man looks like a professor.' See how right I was!"

The captain of the *Clipper* is the strong, silent type; he directs the crew mostly with hand gestures, a jerk of his head, and only an occasional word. He is built solid and has a dark, frowning face.

When I stepped aboard, I greeted him with a sprightly «*Bom dia, capitão!*» He managed a stern smile and a responsive nod. Yes, he is as serious and taciturn as an Indian. What goes on in his mind is not easy to find out. He knows plenty, I think, but he says little.

Our host and guide for the cruise is a wiry but sturdy man of middle-age named Francisco. He gathered our group in the *Clipper's* dining room, served us *caipirinhas*, and oriented us to the boat, the route, and our excursions and activities ahead. We'll be cruising about 250 miles of the Rio Negro, a main tributary of the Amazon, along its course upriver from Manaus.

As the other passengers were unpacking and exploring the *Clipper*, I engaged Francisco in a little get-acquainted talk. I told him that I had lived in the *nordeste*, where, «*Lá, eles falam cantando.*» ('There they speak in a singsong.') Francisco had met some *nordestinos*; he acknowledged the accuracy of my characterization.

Given the clientele he serves, Francisco is more-or-less polyglot, but I hope to communicate with him as much as I can on his, rather than my own, terms, in

Portuguese. We talked further about the indigenous peoples of the Amazon, of which Francisco himself is one, although miscegenated. ...

A bright, sunny day, a stiff breeze, looming clouds, but no rain in sight. The *Amazon Clipper* asserted herself against the current of the Rio Negro, and so began our fluvial explorations.

* * * * *

At dusk tonight, we all donned life jackets and got into the motorized canoe for a cayman-spotting excursion.

I asked Francisco about the difference between a cayman and an alligator. He made distinctions of color, markings, cranial form, and dentition, but, after listening to his explanation, I concluded that the difference between a cayman and an alligator was more significant to the taxonomist than to the night-hunter. It was all *jacaré* to me.

When I lived in Penedo, fishermen would occasionally bring in a live *jacaré*, caught in the Rio São Francisco, to be sold at so much the meaty meter. One restaurant in town had *jacaré* on its menu; I tried it once, as I have tried almost everything in the Brazilian experience at least once. When I returned to the States and regaled my family with my Peace Corps adventures, I was asked what alligator tasted like. "Crocodile," I answered.

Anyway, Francisco played the tropical version of Nature Norm, as he guided us into the lairs.

He was equipped with a battery-powered spotlight for the general search and a miner's light on his baseball cap for the close-in pursuit. As we motored along, Francisco swept the spotlight along the brushy shoreline. He would occasionally spot the tops of trees, too. Which set me to wondering. If he spotted an alligator up in a tree, then we would really be seeing a wonder-of-Nature.

Whenever Francisco's spotlight was reflected by water-level eyes, the helmsman would motor us straight toward the lurking cayman. Francisco would hack away with a machete at the brush and vines that obstructed his view. Then he'd scan the depth of a few feet of dark shoreline water for the reptile.

It reminded me of a turtle or frog hunt at summer camp during my boyhood. You find one in the shallows, position the boat between the quarry and the escape route, then grab the critter.

Not many caymans or alligators about tonight, unfortunately. Was our motor too noisy, or have the locals eaten them all?

Just a few times we saw the red glint of the cayman's eyes reflect Francisco's spotlight. By the time we motored over there, the cayman had vanished into the murk. We seemed in futile pursuit of night-phantoms.

Once, Francisco put a foot over the boat into the mud and readied his noose, which was at the end of a stout pole (no, not at the end of the South Pole). But, as he made his move, the little cayman scooted off.

Francisco spotted a fer-de-lance in a tree. The helmsman cut the throttle so that Francisco could show the big snake to us. So that was what his aerial searchlight was up to.

The tree stood in the water. The helmsman wanted us to get a good look at the fer-de-lance, so he drew us close to the trunk of the tree. If we gave the tree a good hard bump, I worried, we might dislodge the snake and launch it into our laps. Then what a panicked abandon-ship there would be. As the jaws of the *jacaré* in the water have their teeth, so the fer-de-lance packs poison in its viper fangs.

We continued on our hunt.

I heard some big splashes and the fall of a tree, but Francisco was oblivious to those, so intent was he to prove himself the cayman-hunter. We spotted a few more, but, upon our approach, every single one of them vanished.

I was less involved in the task-at-hand than in the aura of the scene. Nature Norm felt some of the old explorer spirit, as we floated amidst the nocturnal life of the tropics.

Rain now threatening and dinner waiting, we headed back to the *Clipper*. Alligator hunt a failure, but Francisco did not apologize or make excuses. Things went like that sometimes. The creatures of the wild are not under contract to put on a nightly show for the tourists.

We all ate ravenously the dinner ready upon our return to the *Clipper*. Brazilian spaghetti, beef and potatoes, rice, bread. Adequate to the purpose.

A good strong coffee to finish the meal, and this entry to finish the day.

I'm mighty glad I came!

Thursday, March 16. The *Clipper*.

I happened to wake up at 3:00 A.M. I looked out the cabin window. Full moon over the Amazon! . . .

On our pre-breakfast excursion by canoe, we visited a bankside squatter.

The young man had given up the mass anonymity of urban poverty in Manaus for the elbow-room solitary independence of rural poverty on the Rio Negro. He was not a pioneer, but an economic refugee.

He lived alone in a wood shack raised on stilts to a level above any anticipated rising of the river. He had felled all the trees in front of his shack. His lawn consisted of tree stumps on a once-greensward trampled into sunbaked mud by his livestock.

He had a typical barnyard assortment—pigs, chickens, ducks, goats, dogs, and (untypical) a lone peacock. Raising pigs in Amazônia is a risky venture, for, just behind any clearing, hidden in the dense undergrowth, lurks the jaguar.

The farm menagerie came a-runnin', as the young man arrived with a canoefull of *mandioca* to feed them. He flung the pieces of tuber ashore, and his animals squabbled over their breakfast, all except for the dogs, who disdained manioc and instead ran about sniffing the chickens, who, vulnerable and distracted by the eating of their breakfast, might easily have become the dogs', had the master not been there to monitor the feeding frenzy.

Francisco made small talk with the young man, as we tourists gawked and took photos of picturesque poverty.

On our way back to the *Clipper*, we heard, above the noise of the motor, loud music blaring from every hovel and hamlet. Even in the Amazon, you cannot get away from that. Everywhere on earth is the cacophony of the human self-assertion against Nature and the Universal Silence. Eventually, we will drown Nature out.

The *Clipper* made its own impact upon the environment. When we got back aboard for breakfast, I happened to look over the side, where I saw a huge oil slick oozing out of the hull.

I pointed it out to the mechanic on the crew, who informed me that the slick was due to a defective water pump. 'It always does that,' he said to reassure me.

Well, why not fix it?, I an American would ask.

No one on the crew showed any concern about the oil slick or enough revulsion to induce pulling of the anchor and motoring upstream or downstream away from the slick. No, we are complacent about our polluting effects. We float unconcerned in the midst of them.

* * * * *

After breakfast, we took a long hike *para a selva* ('into the jungle').

The vegetation was very dense, not much penetration of sunlight, due to the cover of the canopy. A trail had been cut, there wasn't much difference in elevation along it, the air was humid but not oppressive, our pace was leisurely, so the hike wasn't very strenuous.

Considering we were in the deeps of the jungle, there

were surprisingly few bugs. A few iridescent butterflies in the rare sunny glades were conspicuous. As we found out last night on our cayman hunt, there are no mosquitoes in this area. *«O Rio Negro não tem mosquitos»*, Francisco informed us. Probably because, as I read somewhere, the high acidity of the river's water inhibits mosquitorial reproduction.

Back on the *Clipper*, I had had some dealings with insects. While I was unpacking in my cabin yesterday, I discovered that a nest of sugar-eating ants was already in residence.

I didn't bother much about my diminutive cabin-mates, even though the stowaways conducted their foraging for food all over my bunk.

I only remembered today that I had some mints and wrapped candies in one of my bags. Sure enough, the nautical ants had found the cache. They were very enterprising raiders to detect wrapped candy.

I threw the package of candy, crawling with pirates, into the wastebasket.

Later, that seemed to me a waste, so I pulled the package out of the wastebasket and examined it to see whether I might salvage a few pieces. The ants were still in the package but not on every single wrapped piece.

I poured the pieces into my hand and brushed the scurvy knaves off. The unplundered pieces I pocketed for my own later consumption.

Inside one wrapped piece, I discovered four dead ants, stuck fast to their gummy treasure. See what happens to the intemperate and greedy.

Now, on our walk through the jungle, I began eating the pieces of candy, more to savor victory over my adversaries than to find satisfaction in sugar. ...

Not only can Francisco tell you the local Indian lore of the plants, but also the Latin nomenclature. Combining indigenous experiential knowledge with European scientific taxonomy, Francisco knows Amazônia bottom-up and top-down.

He pointed out plants familiar by name—quinine, curare, mahogany trees. There was a tremendous variety of plants, I forget how many hundred kinds of trees alone. Many trees extend their trunks outward in buttresses, to stabilize themselves on a shallow soil where roots grip but feebly. We stopped at the foot of one towering dotard that was, some botanist had informed Francisco, between 600 and 700 years old. Will it be chopped down tomorrow afternoon?

Francisco cut and dispensed palm hearts for us to sample. Palm hearts were a delicacy in my Peace Corps diet, although I obtained them processed and canned, not directly from the tropical earth.

Francisco showed us a stalk that looked like sugarcane; when cut through, it drips fresh water onto your tongue. You could survive on that, if lost or stranded. Not all the plants were for sampling, of course; there were plenty of poisonous ones beneath our feet.

I found it interesting that Francisco talked about the plants mostly in terms of their uses—this one for diarrhea, that one a good diuretic, another one a source of cordage, that tree for high-quality plywood, and so on. Nature seems justified only by her utilitarian properties. What we want to know most about Nature is usage. Human self-interest is the strongest argument, perhaps the only really convincing argument, on behalf of conservation. We should save the Amazonian rainforest, just in case there might be some hitherto undiscovered medicine in one of its plants; let's not burn down the medicine-chest.

Francisco is in favor of use-as-needed; how else would his Indian forbears have survived? He is also in favor of preservation of the whole; how else would his Indian forbears have survived? There is a native conservation ethic, and Francisco has it; it is his religion.

Francisco is as economically, as he is ecologically, sophisticated. He's wise to the Japanese. They'd cut down all the trees in Brazil and haul them off to Japan, pick the whole country clean end to end, he said. Yes, he's wise to the Japanese.

At the end of the trail, we stopped off to visit a *caboclo* household. (*Caboclo* used to mean a person of mixed Indian blood; now it designates any poor rustic.) Our *Clipper* excursion has some local color as a component of the tropical spectrum of Nature.

The children of this family were dark and shy, silly or very serious, One boy, about eleven, found amusement in playing hide-and-seek with a kitten; he burst out laughing like a baby every time the kitten stuck its face out. His younger brother was intent and undistracted, as he worked to untangle his hopelessly tangled mess of fishing line. A girl, about twelve, soon to be beautiful, stood protected behind a split door and stared out at us.

We all sat down on benches outside the front door. The *dona da ca*sa (lady of the house) exchanged a few pleasantries with Francisco and Neilde. The captain of the *Clipper*, come to pick us up at the end of the trail, also appeared. As usual, he was present but non-communicative.

Francisco sent one of the boys to fetch something. The boy returned with a wood bowl full of nuts. *Castagnas,* Brazil nuts, of course! The tourists expect the stereotypical, they ask for it, and so they are served.

I don't like Brazil nuts; they're like eating a rancid candle. I never ate Brazil nuts while I lived in Brazil. But when Francisco handed me my sample, I did eat it, pretending it was a welcome and novel experience.

* * * * *

Francisco's mother was a Sicilian from Palermo. Somehow, she found herself part of a Salesian missionary group that was dispatched to Brazil to try to convert the Indians of the Amazon. It was the impressionable Italian girl who found the Indians impressive. Instead of propagating the gospel, she went native and began to propagate in a more Brazilian manner.

She was only fourteen, when she met a seventeen-year-old Indian man. No matter how much her Christian compatriots might have censured the attraction, they had to legitimize a match that was already made in the minds of the two young people. The couple was quickly married. Such an early start proved fecund, for Francisco is one of the fifteen Sicilian-Indian offspring of that union.

Francisco himself has produced a mere third of his parents' output.

You might think that Francisco leads a narrow life in a remote existence. In fact, he is cosmopolitan, made so by the thirty years of his job as a guide on the Amazon.

Adventurers, researchers, scientists, and tourists from all the significant countries show up dockside for his services. The Amazon is a glamor-spot on the earth; it is Nature at her most explicit, almost Nature pornographic. Francisco has no need to go anywhere to learn about the world; representatives of that world will line up to teach him.

Unlike the missionaries, the clients of the *Clipper* do not come specifically to do Francisco some good. No, they are on a self-seeking quest—to collect a particular rare specimen before it becomes extinct, to photograph Indians (without any Chicago Bulls caps, if possible), to document the destruction of the rainforest, gather evidence, draw up the indictment of the Brazilians, and so on. Nonetheless, Francisco benefits incidentally. The great universities of the world have sent their best people, to learn from Francisco, yes, but also to teach him. As a consequence, he is as well informed as any of the best educated.

Francisco has become a critic and keen valuator of customs and mores. Against Brazilian *machismo*, for example, he believes in the equality of the sexes, appreciates his wife, and practices tolerant and enlightened child-rearing.

A moralist, he is dismayed by the recent social deterioration in Brazil, especially the narcotics trafficking and the violence. He doesn't give his children any spending money, he told me; he's afraid that they'll spend it on glue to sniff.

Francisco's problems as a father in the Amazon

seem little different from those of a father in Chicago or Detroit. A pernicious aspect of globalization is an epidemic of social pathology. Francisco's children pick up nihilism from imported rock music and movies. What can Francisco do about such encroachments upon his parental influence?

There were some advantages to the former Amazonian remoteness and isolation; at least a father could control his children and shield them.

But now Francisco is gnawed by frustration and a feeling of helplessness. When he's away at work, what are his children up to? He has no choice but to leave his children back in civilization.

* * * * *

This afternoon, we took a canoe for some piranha fishing.

As we motored down the stream, I saw a pair of river dolphins breaching. The dolphins of the Amazon seem much smaller than their Mediterranean cousins, but they are just as dolphiny in their behavior.

A few minutes later, I was startled to spot a dolphin that was as pink as a ribbon on a baby girl. A pink dolphin! The circus had suddenly come to the wilderness.

The helmsman cut the motor. We drifted along shore, until Francisco threw a rope across an overhanging branch and tied it to hold us in the current. We would fish close to the shore, in the shade, very convenient and comfortable.

Well, I thought to myself, fishing, here is something I

know something about.

We were issued handlines and a bowl of bloody beef chunks, *carne* for the carnivores.

Tossing my bait into the current, giving it a few provocative twitches, and feeling the line with forefinger and thumb for the gnawing, I caught three piranhas in short order. Behind me, the helmsman, not to be outdone, soon caught four, including what was to be the only big one. We took a firm grip on the piranhas, as we very carefully removed our hooks from their jagged-toothed jaws.

Not much was to be heard from the rest of the boat, even though my shipmates were fishing in the same stream. Francisco, in the bow and in-the-know on technique, did catch one or two, along with some little catfish (*peixe-gato*, the same feline similarity recognized in Portuguese).

We were scheduled to have piranha for dinner tonight, a piranha soup, but, given our catch, I didn't think it would be a hearty one. My three were all small.

I got the impression that they had fished that spot before, perhaps fished out the big piranhas. I may have arrived on the scene at the time of diminishing returns.

How universal fishing humor is. When I tossed a runt piranha back, I said in Portuguese, translated here: "Go get your father and send him to me." Francisco and the helmsman both laughed. The latter made a few jocose fishing remarks that would have been said the same in English.

Trades and avocations are intermediaries. Share one with someone from another country and culture, and you will find some common ground with him. Fishing is one of the most comradely of human activities.

* * * * *

At dusk, it was off again in the pursuit of *jacaré*. The Italian lady, having taken fright at the fer-de-lance looming over our heads last night, declined to join the party.

The new area we explored—backwaters among islands—showed more reptilian retinal glints than last night's hunting ground. Nonetheless, once again they proved easier to see than to catch.

Tonight, I sat in the back with the helmsman, instead of in the bow with Francisco, where I was on our first hunt. The problem, as I saw it, was that we barrelled up on the caymans too fast, spooking them before our arrival. Patience and stealth the issue. But I kept my counsel.

We spotted and pursued for an hour or more. To tell the truth, I had little interest in molesting crocodilians.

Francisco held his noose forward in readiness, but no cayman cooperated by slipping his snout through it.

Francisco was able to grab a tiny one by hand. He passed it among us for inspection. I thought that toothy tyke would have to be our consolation prize.

It was well dark already, but Francisco persisted. At last, he made a lunge and noosed a big one. It thrashed about beside the canoe, twisting and spinning and snapping, despite the noose. Unable to cut the rope, the *jacaré* then tried to bite the pole in half.

All unavailing. The *jacaré* was firmly secured, captured, the autonomy of its living suspended.

The helmsman made his way past us to the bow to assist Francisco in tying the creature's jaws to ineffectualness, trussing it, and hauling it aboard, an unnecessary and unwarrantedly risky procedure, I thought.

The *jacaré* was longer than it was substantial, nearly six feet but only perhaps thirty pounds, a scrawny specimen between his incisors and the tip of his tail.

Francisco announced that we would take it back to the *Clipper*, but just to examine and photograph, then release, the killing and eating of caymans now forbidden. It is an endangered species, so relentless has been the appetite of the locals for its flesh. Most of the manatees of the Amazon, too, have disappeared down human gullets.

As we motored back, the helmsman, who now had the spotlight in order to chart our course back to the *Clipper* in the dark, instead began scanning the shoreline some more, taking over Francisco's designated role.

What light I myself noticed was the flashes of distant lightning in two separate storms, one of them seemingly on its way toward us. Then it was the nightlight of the *Clipper* that my eyes searched for, and to hell with alligator eyes.

I needn't have worried. We arrived at the *Clipper*, as the storms moved off elsewhere. Back safe aboard.

Francisco and the helmsman transferred the kidnapped cayman to the *Clipper* to be subjected to our close scrutiny. I returned to my room to wash up for dinner.

By the time I came back down, our living trophy had been dropped overboard, returned to its ornery freedom.

Dinner tonight included the piranhas we had caught. One of my piranhas must have been kept after all, because Miranda, she with the sleepy eyes, lovely smile, and a purple ribbon in her lustrous black hair, remarked that I was eating my own fish.

I suppose I was. Instead of in soup, the piranhas had been grilled. Mine was a bit dry, but I liked it well enough. Crappie and bluegill and walleye are all OK, but piranha:—Now there's a fish you can really sink your teeth into. Or vice-versa.

People are not at their most attractive while eating, but Miranda was the exception. She would take a dainty bit of food into her mouth and, with lips pursed, seem to suck, rather than chew. She looked like a goddess or nymph feeding on ambrosia.

During dinner, apropos of nothing, Francisco remarked in Portuguese, translated here: "There are some men who don't like women...." I wondered why he wanted to discuss misogyny. But then he added, "There are a lot of them in Rio de Janeiro."

And Neilde, the Brazilian from Vitória, her arm around the neck of her German *namorado*, added, "And women who like women!"

Francisco and Neilde frowned and shook their heads in wonderment. They couldn't understand such a thing at all. ...

The rain did come, at about ten o'clock, when I was already in bed. I heard the first spatters on the roof, then a harder cascade.

I put on my shorts and went out on deck. Little boys do like to play in the rain. But the rain blew under the roof overhang. I got my legs wet, so I crawled back into bed shivering.

Friday, March 17. The *Clipper.*

Heavy overcast this morning, with light sprinkles.

Our dawn canoe excursion was into an *igarapé* (a flooded backwater). Not much water in it, however. The Andes hasn't contributed its snow lately, Francisco explained.

We used the paddle this time, drifting, slowly, quietly, through the brushy narrows, learning about the vegetation and observing the birds.

I asked Francisco whether he had ever heard the singing of the *uirapurú*, the elusive bird of Amazon legend. Yes, many times, he said. The *uirapurú* sings like a flute. Francisco then imitated its song, very accurately, as I remember from a recording of the *uirapurú* that I brought back with me from Brazil after my Peace Corps service. Our guide is no faker; he knows his stuff.

Francisco told me that the *uirapurú* sings in May or June, so I'm early to hear it. When the *uirapurú* sings, Francisco claimed,—(fancifully, not factually)—, all the other birds gather round and listen to it, to learn and to emulate the mastersinger.

Yesterday, when we approached a flock of green parrots, the sound of the canoe's motor drove them off in a panic. In Nature, you've got to take your time and be quiet; but humans are in a hurry, and noisy too.

Today, propelled by our silent paddle, we got closer to some parrots, but they flew off suddenly, screeching their objections to our intrusion. A pair of magnificent macaws flew over us with strong, swift strokes of their wings.

I have always liked the birds of the parrot family, for their beauty, spunk, intelligence, and vocal self-assertiveness. These Amazon parrots will not sit on your shoulder and affectionately nibble your earlobe. They are wild and wary.

As we were hunting *jacaré* last night, some member of the nighthawk family—(the nighthawk, my own totem)—flitted, swooped, and dove for insects rising from the river. This morning's excursion has revealed a toucan's distinctive silhouette against the sky. And I saw an Amazonian variety of kingfisher.

The yellow-rumped *cacique* is one of the most conspicuous and noisy avians hereabouts. The communal flocks of the promiscuous *caciques* raise a ruckus at any approach. Their pendulous nests hang over the river, seemingly exposed but actually protected from predators by colonies of bees or wasps that the *caciques* choose as neighbors. With stinging sentinels always on duty, any snake slithering out a limb licking the air for the warm smell of *cacique* eggs or chicks will regret it.

Unlike the North American lakes and rivers, with their ducks, geese, gulls, and loons, there seem to be few middle-of-the-water floaters in the Amazon. The ever rising and falling shoreline is where the bird action is.

Dipping into the entire palette, Nature has exhausted the spectrum in her haberdashery of the birds of the tropics. Yes, this Amazon is a paradise of birds.

Our quiet drifting in the *igarapé* put Francisco into a romantic mood. He lyricized over the idyll of a hammock between the trees and a bottle of wine cooling in the water. And he joked about the overpopulation problem:

'What else is there to do here?'

The subject of our group conversation then turned to the indigenous peoples of the Amazon. Francisco claimed that, if a white man trespasses upon indigenous territory, the Indians have the right to kill him with impunity. Six missionaries done in last year and eleven the year before, he said.

Francisco alluded to Jívaro headshrinking, even though the Jívaro are far from here, not in Brazil even. He found their ferocious craftsmanship as sensational as we did. He shuddered a bit, then broke the spell with a crack about the shrunken head of a beloved as the best remembrance. Wouldn't that be amorous fetishism to the max? "Yes, I love you for your mind. To prove it, I've hung your head around my neck."

If not headhunting, the Brazilian Indians will at least cut out and eat a piece of the liver of their slain enemy, whether missionary or miner. Venting their spleen on someone else's liver, I suppose you might say.

Francisco is half-Indian himself, remember. Some Indians take to civilization, some don't, he told us. He didn't conclude (although I did) that he belongs to the former group (those who learn the Latin nomenclature of the flora), even while he envies the latter group.

Regarding his natal environment, *Learn about, use, but prescrve* is Francisco's ethic, an ethic that is at the same time indigenous and enlightened-ecological. Francisco may be ambivalent in his allegiance, but his ethnic roots and his education have miscegenated into wisdom.

* * * * *

After breakfast, we put in to a dock, and our group took a walking tour of a river community called Novo Airão.

Against the face of the riverbank, the townspeople had inlaid bricks to spell out, «*Novo Airão. Bemvindos ao Paraíso*» ('Novo Airão. Welcome to Paradise').

The town itself presented the usual dishevelment of tropical habitation. There were some attractive pastel colored houses surrounded by gardens, but otherwise litter and debris everywhere. We walked through the local fish-meat-and-produce market, an experience of intense sensory stimulation.

Their main economic activity, quite suitable to their site, was boatbuilding. The framework of one half-finished project looked like Noah's ark in-the-making.

In the development of their urban infrastructure, they had paved their main street in black asphalt, but most of it had crumbled and washed away downhill in the torrential rains. Whose bright idea was black asphalt under the burning sun and driving downpours? And who paid for the execution of that dumb idea? Not USAID, I hoped.

We popped in to visit a few local households, mostly to examine the fruits, flowers, and vegetables in their gardens. Nature planted all the varieties herself; cultivation improved the array little in my eyes.

Walking through the town, I was taken back to the milieu of my Peace Corps days. Novo Airão was not Penedo, but it had a similar aura. In the town's one-and-only supermarket, I saw a box marked *Penedo*, but it turned out to be the name of some São Paulo manufactory of aluminum cookware. Anyway, seeing the name was like a preview of coming attractions.

Francisco was as familiar with the residents of Novo Airão as with the denizens of the river and jungle. He exchanged greetings with many people along our itinerary.

Some blond children passed us walking down the street; more toward the albino than the blond, actually. The genetic stew of Brazil!

The *dona da casa* of one household we visited was of German stock, she said. Our German tourist aboard stared at her with curiosity. German stock maybe, her appearance Teutonic, yes, but, when she spoke, she was Brazilian through and through. The real Germans turn their heads away in disapproval of any mongrelization.

I liked Novo Airão and found it hospitable. Ah, tropical languor! When you first arrive, you're appalled by the mess of it; but stay just a few months and you'll go native. Going native,—my own temptation, to which I once succumbed as an eager sinner.

Brazil is seductive, even to seducers. The Japanese, however, are probably immune to tropical allure.

* * * * *

Along the shore, as we cruised, I saw a tall tree besieged by an opportunistic vine. The vine had scaled the trunk and now used every square foot of its surface to the vine's own photosynthetic advantage.

Higher up, the vine had extended out the tree's limbs, in a further colonization of available territory to exploit. And so upward, outward, from limbs to branches to twigs, the vine covered all.

At last, at the spread of the canopy, the vine had overlaid most of the tree's leaves, depriving the tree of the sunlight it needs for its own sustenance.

Tendrils of the vine even reached upward from the canopy, into thin air, where there was nothing to grasp and exploit.

What now? The tree is doomed. When its last leaf is put into darkness by the leaves of the vine, the tree will succumb. Then rot, a sudden wind, the break, and collapse into the river, the corpse of the tree pulling down and drowning its nemesis. The end will be death, extinction, for the exploited first, then for the exploiter.

Now, there's an ecological allegory of the human race for you. ...

While I'm on the subject of trees:

I saw a dead tree standing on the shoreline, its gaunt trunk white with death, its remaining self-extension a mere fork of two limbs at its top.

On one limb of the bare arboreal skeleton, high up, a leafy plant had availed itself of a bony perch.

And there on the plant, in the sun, was a brilliant red flower, its petals opened, bright against the white of the dead tree. That flower was gorgeous in its solitariness, even though it bloomed atop death and decay.

Well, there's another allegory for you: The allegory of *the beautiful soul.*

* * * * *

This afternoon, the *Clipper* pulled into a stretch of white sand beach. The program called for swimming and beachcombing.

It has been overcast and windy all day. Despite the weather and the dire threat of schistosomiasis in any fresh water, I decided to add to my lifelong natatory itinerary (to the Great Lakes, Atlantic, Pacific, and Mediterranean) the fluvial Amazon. So in I went. The river bottom was sandy and free of debris, the water of the Rio Negro coffee colored and warm.

I swam around, not too venturesome toward the deeps and dispelling thoughts of horrors of piranhas. The swimming was easy, as I was buoyed up by the warm water.

Only the Barcelonan man and I had availed ourselves of the opportunity to swim; Miranda waded a bit, washing her bare feet.

After a half-hour I came ashore to join the rest of the group for beachcombing. Miranda took a photo of me, smiled, and watched me as I emerged from the river.

Granules of gold sometimes wash ashore here, Francisco told us to pique our interest in the beachcombing. But we found only broken bottles, tin cans, and paper litter.

Some trees on the beach had been burned by picnickers; Francisco shook his head at such mindless destruction. He showed us one fallen tree that had been stripped of its bark, by some girl who brewed a chemical abortion from the bark, Francisco surmised.

I wish I understood the other half of all that Francisco is telling us. He'll start out in Italian, switch to Spanish for a few sentences, throw in some German words, revert to his native Portuguese, then wind up in English. He's trying to be host and guide to the heterogeneous group of us, but his linguistic dexterity sometimes leaves me a language or two behind.

Well, after twenty-five years of my Portuguese cast into silence and my Italian too loaded with decades of rust, it's not surprising that my current comprehension should be wanting. Nonetheless, I've learned a lot about the Amazon these past few days, by the looking as much as the hearing, by the direct experience as well as the explanations.

We reboarded the *Clipper*, cruised a bit, then got into the canoe for some more local sociology. We stopped to visit another bankside family, their house too on stilts against the seasonal rising of the waters.

A mangy dog, half-featherless chickens, the usual litter.

The man of the house was at the shore, getting ready to fish for *tucunaré* (peacock bass). Could I join him?, I was ready to plead.

His belly was distended, not with the usual gravity of age, but, I think, with some parasite from a meal served to him by his wife.

She had the haggard look of excessive childbearing. Seven of them were to be counted around the house. Bronzed, beautiful faces; precocious nubility in the girls.

Grandfather shuffled into the room coughing. He settled into a hammock and started swinging it like a boy, just for the joy of the motion.

The family had some crafts to sell—necklaces of seedpods and bones, woven hats, carved coconuts, and such. I lent the German five *reais* to buy an item he wanted. None of it appealed to me.

My attention was directed toward the family and their domestic environment, until I was distracted by a huge hairy tarantula-like spider that walked boldly down the middle of the room.

Francisco and the *dona da casa* examined and discussed a new TV the family had acquired. Battery powered, of course; no juice lines here.

The woman couldn't get the TV to work, she complained to Francisco. He studied the manual, then told her that she needed a UHF antenna. I looked out at the VHF antenna mounted on a wood pole. Maybe it needed a ground, I speculated. Anyway, they might be out of range of the transmission from Manaus. I had seen satellite-dishes in Novo Airão; the family should buy one of those and tune in to the world, any old sitcom rerun to get their minds off their oppressive environment.

What would the family do all day and all night without a TV to help them while away the tedium of their lives in the tropics?

Then it was out back to witness a demonstration of rubber-tapping. Francisco cut a diagonal furrow across the tree, just below earlier furrows. Immediately, the white latex sap flowed down through the groove. Francisco caught the flow in a can, the top of which he had bent and forced into the bark.

That particular type of exploitation of Nature was what earned the fortunes to build the mansions and the Opera House of Manaus. But then an Englishman smuggled some rubber tree seeds out of Brazil and set up a more efficient plantation in a British colony in Asia. Later, the Americans skipped Nature altogether—(or, at least, recent Nature)—by deriving a synthetic rubber from petroleum.

Today, the tapping of natural rubber continues but is mostly an obsolete enterprise, a technological curiosity, one of the many quaint activities to entertain the tourists in Amazônia.

As Francisco was concluding the brief demonstration by showing us balls of raw latex, the German suddenly began jumping up and down and swatting his legs. Intent upon learning about rubber, he had carelessly stepped upon an ants' nest. They, unsympathetic to his desire to learn, sent out the troops to repel him. The German brushed off the ants from under his trousers, frantically, as Neilde helped, each of them conducting a counterattack on one leg. We all then retreated from flowing rubber and swarming ants.

Did the bites sting?, the Italian asked the German.

Yes, Helmut admitted, but he brushed off his admission of pain as gingerly as he had brushed off the ants.

Saturday, March 18. The *Clipper;* Manaus.

On our pre-breakfast canoe excursion, we stopped at a local tourist trap.

The whole was a floating dock, with open-air restaurant, dance pavilion, and a raft of souvenir stalls. We were the first party to arrive this day. The proprietor and the vendors were standing around, half-asleep.

They had a miserable menagerie there: A tapir that walked around eating plastic wrappers, a sullen cayman in a boxed pool of water, an anaconda coiled in slime and its own cast-off skin, two macaws who were exercising their beaks by chewing off pieces of a corrugated roof, and a flea-bitten, scratching, squirrely squirrel monkey who would jump on you and clamber up your body to pick your pockets. The jungle as tawdry as its human residents.

Our group walked out on a rotting wooden plank bridge erected high over the mud. More souvenir stalls, these empty, the length of the bridge.

The attraction on the other side was the Lago de Janauario, more swamphole than lake.

The picturesque feature of the Lago de Janauario is the giant *Victoria regia* water lily. There were a few white blossoms, but many of the lily pads seemed deceased and in process of decomposition. Well, the jungle must have morbidity with its vitality.

I spotted a small cayman in the water—(where's your noose now, Francisco?)—and some fish that swam in lazy circles. A hawk flew back and forth over the *lago*, looking for its breakfast. And a little stilt-legged bird walked daintily from pad to pad picking off bugs.

Francisco showed us a stalk with a bulbous tip, a phallic symbol in local lore, he said. It didn't take much symbolic imagination to make that association, I thought. The stalk reminded me of the phallic mushroom that made Thoreau wonder whether Nature had turned dirty-minded. Francisco further informed us that the stalk was used by pregnant Indian women as a talisman to insure the birth of a male child, and that the vulgar nickname for the stalk was 'gift for a widow'.

Miranda, our honeymooner, asked Francisco to hold the stalk up for her. She then proceeded to videotape it. Why she wanted to videotape a plant without motion was a mystery to me, not to mention the public indelicacy of the symbolism under her present biographical circumstances. When she finished shooting, Miranda gave a shy smile of satisfaction to herself. Francisco dropped the stalk from the bridge, down into the mud below.

* * * * *

The food on the *Amazon Clipper* has been quite good. Ariete, the cook, endures a sweltering work environment in the little kitchen in the stern, but she skilfully and efficiently turns out savory plates in good time.

Francisco mentioned that a client of the boat, an American, once tried to induce Ariete to come to the United States to be his private cook, but she shrugged him off. She's apparently content as a master chef of Amazonian itineraries.

I remarked to the Italian that, on a trip of this sort, the two most important people were the guide and the cook. In Francisco and Ariete, we have been well served.

On the *Clipper*, I enjoyed black-beans-and-rice again, no matter how much I used to bemoan the monotony of it in my Peace Corps diet. Ariete served spaghetti as a side dish a lot, but you never get tired of spaghetti.

The main dishes have been typically Brazilian—grilled fish and chicken and roast beef. Ariete has prepared various types of salads and cooked vegetables too. Eggs, not just rolls, for breakfast. Cornbread and a rolled *tortilla* (or whatever it's called in Amazônia). Only the sandwich bread was tasteless (store-bought, probably).

I love the sweetness and savor of the tropical fruits: Papaya, bananas—(Brazil produces more than twenty varieties)—, guava, passion fruit, pineapples, mangoes, melons. Ariete even served us fried bananas sweetened with brown sugar and seasoned with cinnamon, reminding me of that sweet treat I myself brought back from Brazil to Chicago.

We had *doce* too, another item I ate a lot of when I lived in Brazil. *Doce* is just a slice of too-sweet fruit gelatin, but, complement it with coffee, and it's a perfect punctuation to a meal.

—By the way, regarding coffee in Brazil:---It should be served, the locals say, 'black as sin, strong as lust, sweet as revenge, and hot as hell'.—

On leaving the *Clipper*, I was cffusive in my praise of Ariete, first rehearsing what I wanted to say to her. She looked pleased. I joked by inviting her to come back to the States to be *my* private cook. Ariete smiled and declined with a little blush and a shake of her head.

Enjoying a woman's cooking for a few days is like an

amorous affair. She doesn't serve up her body, true, but she nourishes your body and its erotic energy. Not all love feeds so well as food.

* * * * *

After breakfast, we cruised to the so-called Meeting of the Waters, where the Rio Negro and the Rio Solimões converge to form the designated Amazon.

The Negro and the Solimões are quite different rivers, the former tinged dark but otherwise clear, the latter yellow, turbid, muddy.

Their *meeting* proves an incompatible one, for the two rivers come together but do not mingle their waters. Instead, beneath the green floating mats of aquatic vegetation and debris carried along, the yellow Solimões swirls and billows around the waters of the Negro, the two rivers now intertwined in a standoffish dance.

The Italian compared the colors to black coffee and coffee-with-milk, not really apt, because, when mixed, coffee and milk instantly adopt some uniform color in proportion to the mix.

Not so the Rio Negro and the Solimões. It is only many miles downstream that their aversion to each other wears down, and they blend at last, like incompatible spouses who, after many years of strife, just get used to, and abide, each other. A bad match, but become inevitable by gravity and time. ...

Our cruise coming to an end, we sailed past the waterfront of Manaus. A more bustling, colorful, and squalid scene you couldn't imagine.

The variety of boats alone would take a long

description: Crudely carved wooden canoes, brightly painted double-decked passenger ferries, huge barges transporting natural gas—(if they exploded, you'd think they would create a tidal wave)—, floating gasoline stations, a floating post office, a luxury liner come from Holland, a three-masted schooner, rusting steel hulks serving as who-knows-what, a jet ski, and so on, a steady passing traffic. Everybody just pitches their trash overboard, so it was not only boats and ships that come floating by.

On the shore: The rails and ramps and derricks to pull up watercraft for overhauling, the fish market, wharves, warehouses, the water purification plant (suspect), black, rusted industrial structures, huge silver tanks, petroleum processing, natural gas, chemicals. A lot going on, with an overall disconcerting effect.

Manaus has nearly a million people now. My guidebook describes the city as "dirty, ugly, and crime ridden". If I translated that summary judgment *«sujo, feio, e cheio de crime»,* I wonder how the Manaus Chamber of Commerce would respond. I'll take the city tour in a day or two and form my own judgment.

My shipmates will be off in different directions: The Italian couple to São Paulo, Buenos Aires, and Montevideo, three metropolises in three different countries; the German and his Espírito Santo *namorada* to Belém, Salvador, and Ilheus, all within Brazil; the Barcelonans home to Spain, where, their honeymoon over, their marriage will begin.

I'll be on to the *nordeste* for my nostalgia trip, but meanwhile Manaus.

I bid farewells to my shipmates, to Francisco, the

captain and crew. I checked back into the Hotel Tropical.

Owned by Varig, the Brazilian national airline, the Tropical is a luxury resort hotel, like those I know in Maui. The Tropical has 600 rooms and a staff of a thousand. Laid out in a rectangular inward-facing cloister—(maybe you don't really want to know where you are, in the *jungle*!)—, it is virtually self-contained, with bars and restaurants, a shopping center, athletic areas, a ballroom, convention facilities, pools and fountains. There is a lot of rich dark wood inside and tropical landscaping outside. Prices for meals and merchandise are sky-high, of course. They even impose a huge mark-up on postage stamps.

Like the Hawaiian resorts, the Tropical is a place for couples, not for a solo vagabond; but I chose it for its convenience in making the connection with the *Amazon Clipper*, which docks virtually on the Tropical's threshold. I would just have to make do with all the self-indulgent luxury.

My first afternoon in the Tropical, I visited its mini-zoo. It is was planned and laid out, with spacious cages among shaded, winding walkways. The zoo offered an indigenous assortment. Wild parrots flew over the heads of their incarcerated cousins. There were toucans and tortoises, caymans and capybara, several varieties of perverted monkeys, a puma, and even three jaguars. One jaguar was very obese, but that's the modern civilized sedentary life-of-leisure for you.

I had been so lulled by the absence of mosquitoes that, while on shore excursions from the *Clipper*, I never once applied the insect repellant I had brought with me. Oblivious carelessness on my part, for, as I walked the zoo paths in my shorts, my legs itched from purple welts, some of them oozing a drop of water from their centers, where, perhaps, I scratched them with a sharp fingernail.

Back in my room I took an inventory—54 bites. I thought when I first began scratching that it might be fleas from that mangy dog at the last hovel-on-the-bank we had visited or perhaps something in the sand of the beach. Unlike the German with his ants, I detected no attack in progress, but I bore the direct hits. Purple welts, all below the waist, reminiscent of the wood ticks of the Quetico. Yes, that's it, I think I've been ticked off, 54 times.

What made me so complacent as to think there would be no *bichos* in the jungle? They had the unchallenged best of me, those *bichos*. Well, only the inhabitants of Novo Airão live under the self-deceptive delusion that the jungle is paradise.

* * * * *

The toilets in the Hotel Tropical are the most inefficient and wasteful of water that I have ever seen. Plumbing profligacy.

The flush is a button on the wall. You press it, and a roar of rushing, foaming water charges into the bowl, with such force and volume that a veritable waterspout is raised up by the turbulence. It's almost a parody of the Roman *gioco d'acque* or the vertical fountains of Tivoli.

The flush continues in a great, noisy riot of spinning and surging and bubbling and upwelling of water, until you are reaching for your life jacket.

Suddenly, it stops, there is a guttural gulp, and the

flush is completed. Not successfully, however. A backflow from the trap might leave some of the deposit behind.

You flush again, and you notice that a little spritz comes out of the poorly sealed button-valve on the wall, onto your back if you're still seated, into your face if you examine the valve too closely, or, otherwise, into the air over the toilet.

Of course, this is Amazônia. What is a waste of water here, where there is the greatest volume of flowing freshwater on the surface of the earth?

Nonetheless, I like a well-engineered functionality. In the toilets of the Hotel Tropical, the removal of waste is itself wasteful. They resort to an Amazonian inundation, where a focused flow would suffice to accomplish the task.

Sunday, March 19. Manaus.

Seeking to pile my pleasures and exhaust my days with thrills, as usual, I tried to arrange a daylong excursion to fish for *tucunaré*. (I was provoked by some huge fresh-caught *tucunaré* I saw in the fish market of Novo Airão.) Then, in the evening, if possible, I might attend some show at the Teatro Amazonas, the Opera House of Manaus.

On such short notice and with the few days I'll be here in Manaus, it wasn't possible to arrange the fishing expedition. Good thing, as it turned out, because a chill I had been feeling on the *Clipper* was becoming a bad cold that left me with no other ambition than to lie in bed. Further exposure to the Amazonian environment would have done me no good. Had I gotten skunked in the fishing, it would have been even worse.

I was taking aspirins, to little effect, so I went to the drugstore in the Tropical, where the clerk (no pharmacist, just some kid clerk) advised me confidently that two of these little pills washed down by a tonic of effervescent vitamin C would fix me right up. They had worked like a charm for him, he assured me.

I took his advice, then wondered whether I should waste the day in convalescence or venture upon some not too rigorous activity or other.

—(Last night, I dreamt that my trip had been cut short, and I was back home in the apartment of my childhood on Draper Street. "But I just started my trip! I want to go back to Brazil!," I protested to my brother. "No, no, you're sick, and you don't have the money to go back there," my brother said. "Stay here, where you belong." And I felt so frustrated, until I woke up in Manaus.)—

After lunch, I perked up, so I thought that I might at least go into town to do some shopping. The Tropical operates a shuttle-bus.

I bought my ticket but misunderstood the schedule I had been given. I thought that *Shopping Center* and *City* meant the same thing, that we would arrive in some downtown *praça* (public square) from which I would walk store to store.

The bus first stopped at a huge, windowless building. Oh, an indoor mall of some sort, I thought. Then I understood that Manaus had both this mall and other shops downtown, more of a retail trade than I had expected.

Manaus is only 3° of latitude from the equator. It was 2:00 in the afternoon, humid, and about 100°. Given my Amazonian indisposition and the weather conditions, I decided to spend the afternoon in the mall, such as it was. No matter what it proved to be, at least I'd keep cool and not aggravate my illness.

I went inside, and it turned out to be the Woodfield Mall of the tropics. Two levels of stores, with shiny escalators and fast-food emporiums, the whole of it sparkling, brand-new, and bustling with the middle class.

The contrast between the riverside hovels I had been visiting from the *Clipper* and this palace of consumerism was stupefying. From the most primitive to the most modern, from abject subsistence to conspicuous excess, from Nature's poverty to civilization's plenty, from just one day to another, but virtually in the same place.

The people in the mall were clean, well dressed, and well-to-do. Not a pitiful sight or pathological symptom to be seen. Well, there was one little girl, stooped over, with a glazed look in her eyes...some nervous system damage; but she was in her Sunday best and being chauffeured from store to store in a deluxe wheelchair. She had her handicap, but she was getting the best of care, no doubt about it.

Now, the rural Brazilians I remember, in the *nordeste* of my Peace Corps days, looked like this: Clothes of ragged rags, dirty unshod feet, matted filthy hair, missing front teeth (due to chewing on raw sugarcane and dental services unavailable or unaffordable), bellies swollen from parasites, legs bowed from rickets, the word *doente* (sick) the most common one in everyone's vocabulary, the crippled, malformed, ill-formed, beggars, the destitute, in short, unfortunates everywhere. None of that in the Shopping Center of Manaus!

I wasn't in Brazil, really; I was in Woodfield Mall in Schaumburg, Illinois. The signs in the store windows were in a different language, but they said the same thing. There was loud music playing—Latin raucousness—, but otherwise no difference.

Every teenage girl in Manaus must have been in that mall on this Sunday afternoon; again, no difference from Woodfield, Oak Brook, Yorktown, or any other Chicago-area mall I have been to.

I seemed to be the oldest person in the mall. I recalled a statistic that 70% of the population of Brazil is under 30 years old. Around me, it was 70% under 25. Well, maybe the shopping mall doesn't portray an accurately representative sample of the population.

Actually, it wasn't so much that I was suddenly returned to the States, or to any other country; I wasn't dislocated at all. I was in the most familiar modern environment, the shopping mall, which is not an exotic location but a common milieu. I was in cosmopolis, at last; its name is consumerism.

On the *Clipper* excursions in the canoe, I sheltered my head from the tropical sun under a Panama hat, which was woven in Ecuador, purchased in the United States, and put to service in Brazil.

Oh, wonders of the world economy! It is now possible for anyone anywhere to buy anything made anywhere else. What a life we moderns enjoy. What more could we possibly want out of life? We can have it all.

And there I was, in the middle of the jungle, in a shopping mall that had it all.

I hate shopping, I confess, but I had committed one afternoon of my life to the Shopping Center of Manaus. It would be three hours before the shuttle-bus to the Hotel Tropical would pass by to fetch me back.

So I made the rounds of the stores, systematically, doggedly, once, twice, resting on a bench and surveying the scene betweentimes. I indulged myself in a banana split. And I did buy something,—a leather purse for Janet, made in Brazil, wherever that is.

The cosmopolis of consumerism: That's where we all live. When we go off somewhere else, we merely find ourselves back in that same cosmopolis. Consumerism is a culture-in-itself, really; it is the only culture most of us have. We've got to buy. That is our participation in culture. Consumption is the very proof of culture.

Monday, March 20. Manaus.

I had a hell of a time getting to sleep last night, due to this sultry climate. The tropical environment, if left as it is, is not congenial to humans.

My room is air-conditioned—the Tropical *is* a five-star hotel, after all—, but too cold air conditioning makes me all stuffed up, especially with my cold. Generally, I can stand heat all right, but high humidity is bad for my bronchials.

My inside environmental strategy since I arrived at the Tropical has been to run the air-conditioner all day, when I am out of the room, to cool and dry everything out, then turn it off at night and sleep in the climate of its accumulated conditioning.

Yesterday, the unit didn't seem to be working right. Was it because, trying to avoid the too cold situation, I had turned up the thermostat, only to disconnect the compressor's drying-out effect? Anyway, at bedtime it was steamy.

My cold made me doubtful of what I should do. The medication prescribed by the kid clerk had tightened up my chest, as much as my sinuses. What would make things better, what worse?

I turned the air-conditioner on. It ran awhile without doing much good, then died abruptly. The room was a suffocating sweatbox, making my breathing and sleeping—(both should go on simultaneously)—difficult.

In desperation, I threw open the window. Outside was just another suffocating sweatbox. No breeze in the Amazon basin that I could detect. I heard a few night sounds of the local creatures, who had no choice but to endure their habitat without five-star amenities.

The window open, at least the barrier between my unbreatheable confinement and the unbreatheable Amazonian expansiveness around me was removed.

I had no other possible recourse, unless it was to join the monkeys on some tree limb. ...

Then, suddenly, it was 7:00 A.M. I had indeed slept and breathed the night away.

I started with the notion of Hell. As the promoter at the devil's tourist agency told a prospective tourist in describing Hell, "Of course it's hot there. But it's a dry heat."

* * * * *

When I wasn't able to sleep last night, I took out a book I had brought with me. It was *Child of the Dark*, the diary of Carolina Maria de Jesus, a *favelada* (slum dweller) of São Paulo.

Dona Carolina had only a second-grade education. Her diary was not so much a literary exercise as a self-administered therapy. I think that she wrote to exert psychological control over a situation in which she lacked economic control. Writing as an attempt to feel in control,—I understand that.

Dona Carolina's diary is an artless work of blunt realism. Filth, disease, perversion, meanness, resentment, and the hopelessness of the underclass are her themes. Her diary has become a primary source for sociologists and reformers, especially in Brazil.

Child of the Dark is more than thirty-five years old.

Whatever righteous outrage over poverty it once stirred up has long since died away, for the *favelas* (shantytown slums) of São Paulo and the other Brazilian cities (including those of Manaus, which I have now seen firsthand) have metastasized through the flesh of the Brazilian urban landscape.

During my twenty-five year absence, the population of Brazil has grown from 90 million to 160 million, an 80% increase. And the population of *favelados*? Much higher, of course, but I wonder whether it is a bigger percentage, as well as a simple increase in gross numbers.

Dona Carolina lived in the midst of beatings, fights, stabbings, and shootings, the random violence of drunken hopelessness. Yet, when she herself was threatened with violence, she would respond, 'Watch out, or I'll put you in my book!.'

Writing as defense, as revenge even.—I can understand that too.

Dona Carolina's counterthreat, I could tell her, is an impotent one. What is the immortal ignominy of the victim of literary calumny, compared to the very dead recipient of a rock to the head or a knife thrust deep into bowels?

Well, *dona* Carolina was a literary success story, anyway. Some journalist out slumming one day discovered her and her diary, edited the latter and got it published, to best-seller results, the biggest best seller in the history of Brazilian publishing, in fact. "It stirred the conscience of Brazil!" Judging by the longterm, maybe not. At least *dona* Carolina got the money to escape her appalling surroundings and say good riddance to her rude neighbors.

While in the *favela*, *dona* Carolina had eked out a living picking up and collecting scrap paper for sale to recyclers. Now, as a published writer, she herself had become a major producer of scrap paper, that is, the tens of thousands of copies of her book that were sold, first in Portuguese in Brazil, then in the English of my U.S. edition, and, I suppose, in other languages elsewhere.

All books are scrap paper in the end. *Dona* Carolina, paper-picker of the slums of São Paulo, had gotten her true revenge on the world at last.

* * * * *

This afternoon, I took the van tour of Manaus, the only practical way to see it, in that the Hotel Tropical is removed from the city, and Manaus itself is a bit chaotic to permit individual exploration on a short-term stay.

Our guide was a young man from Santarém, the other principal city in Amazônia. He is a *crente*, that is, a Protestant, inducted by some Baptists who came down from Texas to proselytize in the jungle. He seems a sweet boy, and so should make a good Christian.

There were only four of us on the tour. The others were a Brazilian woman from São Paulo—(I asked her whether she knew about the diary of *dona* Carolina; of course, she had read all the best sellers)—and a fatuous couple from Barrington, Illinois, of all places.

When the Barrington wife found out that our guide was a Baptist, she enthusiastically identified herself as a Baptist too, but a dancing Baptist, she insisted, not the conventional nondancing one. I had always thought of Baptists as a sect of blacks and poor Southern whites, a very dated conception, as driven home to me by the apparition of an affluent Barrington Baptist.

Upon the revelation of such shared religiosity, I myself became so full of the Spirit that I almost volunteered to dance down for full baptismal immersion in the waters of the mighty muddy Amazon itself, the Jordan being too distant.

First main stop on the tour was the Museum of the Indian, which is operated by the Salesian missionaries. That seemed to me somewhat like the successful hunter showing off his collection of stuffed heads.

The museum consisted of a series of rooms with glass cases filled with dusty artifacts—pottery, basketry, primitive tools, hunting and fishing gear, and so on. Where are the Indians today who know how to make and use such stuff? I saw a photo of Indian children waving Brazilian flags while standing beneath the purview of a nun in front of their school.

One room had a little tropical diorama of stuffed birds and animals of Amazônia; it was a macabre mummification of tropical life. I spotted, on one limb of a desiccate tree, a green-and-yellow, definitely Australian, parakeet. What was it doing there, that alien among the deceased indigenes? Someone's purchased pet perhaps, fraudulently inducted after death into the Brazilian Bird Hall of Fame.

They might as well have rounded up the few scattered Amazonian Indians remaining, stuffed them, and put them in the glass cases of the Museum of the Indian. The technologically naive peoples of the earth are as good as done for.

The bulletin boards of the Museum were posted with newspaper stories about recent atrocities committed against the Indians by prospectors looking for minerals on Indian reservations. The spirit of Latin El Dorado lives on.

The missionaries express their indignation about the murders of Indian bodies, but the missionaries themselves have murdered the Indians' souls. Unlike Francisco's mother, the missionaries would not let themselves be seduced by the Indians. No, the missionaries were right and righteous. They would impose salvation upon the savages, whether the latter wanted it or not. What Herman Melville reported from Polynesia in the nineteenth century, I report from Brazil in the twentieth. The cost of salvation has been extinction. The Indians are saved; the Indians are lost.

Leaving the Museum, we drove past the hillside *favelas*, which I had first spotted from the bus to the Shopping Center. The *favela* shacks are on stilts, against the seasonal incursions of the Amazon waters up the valleys. There are few places in Amazônia where you can be sure of year-round solid dry ground. The *jacaré* is Amazônia's most adapted denizen.

As an urban contrast to the shanties: The Palace of the Governor, built with the money from the exploitation of natural rubber, and Adrianopolis, the neighborhood of the wealthy of Manaus. (The U.S. consulate is in Adrianopolis. Hey, we know what neighborhood we Americans deserve.)

Then to the famous Teatro Amazonas, the Manaus Opera House, which, when you think of it, is one of the strangest ideas imaginable: The opera, the most sophisticated concept of Italian high culture, transplanted into the heartland of natural primitivism.

The Teatro Amazonas was renovated most recently

in 1990, so it was a presentable extravagance. (Next year is its centenary; a big celebration is planned.)

If the cultural concept was European, so, too, were the architecture and furnishings—British wrought iron, Carrara marble, Murano glass chandeliers, French mirrors, and most of the material for the construction shipped over from Europe. What did Brazil contribute to the building? Wood to walk on, local tree corpses.

The auditorium itself is small in area, but has a half-dozen stacked rows of balconies in sweeping curves. Artwork by the Italians, of course. The usual Allegories, bare (white) breasts, and *trompe l'oeil.*

There were, on the rails of the balconies, medallions with the great names of performance art—Aristophanes, Calderón, Molière, Beethoven, Rossini, Schiller—, a heterogenous mix, but mostly Europeans.

Some prominence was given to one local boy, Carlos Gomes, who wrote an opera called *O Guaraní* about...the Indians of Brazil! The name of both composer and his *magnum opus* were already among the trivia in my head, but I never heard tell of the opera being performed, nor can I hum any tune from its score. What must an opera about Indians be like? A Romantic caricature and inadvertent ethnographical farce, I would suspect.

I sat with our guide and the *paulista* lady and enjoyed a bottle of *guaraná* at the opera bar. There will be a pop music show in the Teatro Amazonas tomorrow night, but I'll be gone by then.

The girl who guided us around the building had big beautiful round eyes. (I had joined the *paulista* lady for the Portuguese version of the tour, rather than the Barrington couple for the English version.) The girl, finding out that I was an American, spoke to me slowly, clearly, and with sharp enunciation, as if I were stupid; it helped my comprehension a lot. But it wasn't her voice that kept my attention, as she stared intently at me; it was her eyes. I had trouble dividing my attention between her eyes and that damn distraction of a building.

Back in the van once again, the Barrington lady told me that their guide reported that Luciano Pavarotti had been there a few weeks before and was persuaded to give a private recital to fifty Germans. (Fifty Germans, in Manaus?) When the great tenor arrived in the auditorium, she said, he sounded a loud tone to test the acoustics. The Barrington lady thought that rude, like kicking the tires of a vintage auto. I told her that it seemed reasonable to me for a singer to test the environment in which he'd be working; she pondered my argument, then nodded in acquiescence.

Funny thing was, when I myself first stepped into the auditorium and approached the stage, I then faced the audience (of empty seats) and was tempted to raise my own voice in stentorian song. *"O sole mio"* would be too hackneyed even for an audience of jungle rustics; what about the climactic last lines of *"E lucevan le stelle"*? But it was hopeless. We writers are mere pipsqueaks.

Next stop was the Municipal Market. Another European idea, in its architecture, which was structural steel. The insides, however, were authentic indigenous, pure peasant-local,—tropical fruits and vegetables, raw meat and fish.

It is a bit of a demoralizing shock for an American grocery shopper, like our Barrington lady, to come across meat in its crude reality. No slaughterhouse at a distance or hacking and whacking behind a wall, out of sight. Not even the three layers of shrinkwrap to smother the smell. Nope, in the Manaus Municipal Market, the meat is heaped in bloody piles on the counters, the flies claiming first dibs.

We arrived at the Market toward the end of the operating day, so most of the buying and selling was over. There were fish still to be had, including a few tantalizing *tucunaré* that I myself had wanted to snatch, not dead from a filthy counter but alive from the waters of the Rio Negro. Would the chef at the Tropical fry up the fillets for me, if I brought them to him? The vendors were eager to sell these *tucunaré*, for, after this hot day, tomorrow the fish would be putrid.

The *paulista* lady bought some kind of *mandioca* flour that, she said, was unavailable in São Paulo. The vendor just guessed at the weight he sold her. When we were leaving the market, she was pleased to find out at the certified scale that the vendor had been either generous or unskilled in his estimate of accurate weight.

Down to the waterfront we went. There was a big gray military ship there. (By the way, Manaus has a training center for jungle warfare, whether that warfare is *in* the jungle or *against* the jungle depends on how you choose to translate the name of the place. Regimes from all over Latin America have sent their commandoes there to train for any eventual insurgency of revolutionaries.)

The docks were crowded with boats of all kinds, especially the double-decked passenger ferries, where sleeping accommodations are the rails from which you hang your hammock. Many people evidently arrive the day before sailing, string up their hammocks on the docked boat, and so save the cost of a night in a hotel.

With all the loiterers, as well as those unloading and loading freight, the docks were noisy and crowded.

Our guide happened to know a crew member on one of the boats—a fellow Baptist—, so we were invited aboard for a look-see. There were several levels of open deck space, capacity 377 people, a little bar on the top. As a trip to the various river towns of the Amazon may last several days, you could really make some new friends, though I doubt you'd get much sleep.

A poster on the boat exhorted passengers not to litter the river, yet even the crew was illiterate to that message. There doesn't seem to be much sentimentality about the Rio Negro, let alone any ecological sensitivity or custodial responsibility, or even that ultimate argument that I mentioned before, namely, human self-interest. It'll all just flow downstream. Let the people of Belém deal with it.

Manaus has its reminiscences of Calcutta, but, all in all, it's a vibrant city, especially given the tropical lassitude you would expect in its inhabitants. I had thought that Manaus would be little more than a wilderness outfitters' post, like Ely or Crane Lake, Minnesota. But, no, it's a full-fledged modern city, with the best and worst of what all major cities have.

Manaus, a heap of manufactured excreta in the midst of Nature's own profligate production. I suppose one day the artifacts of Manaus will be in glass cases, long after the last inhabitant of the city has become extinct.

* * * * *

Oh, let me finish the story about the air conditioning.

I am more inclined to endure than to complain, but Janet had told me that, if anything on my trip was unsatisfactory, I should insist on my rights and not be reluctant to demand the best, as I deserved.

So, after breakfast this morning, I headed to the reception desk to report the problem. I hoped to encounter the young clerk I had first met there, when, before the Clipper cruise, I needed a room at 5:00 A.M. He would now transfer me to another room, one with an operating air-conditioner, I thought.

On the one hand, I hated the bother of packing up, paying a bellboy for a short shuttle, then unpacking, only to have to repack tomorrow morning. On the other hand, I dreaded another night of swelter.

My clerk friend was not at his post. Instead, it was a young woman, who listened to my complaint and merely wrote my room number on a slip of paper.

What would come of that?, I wondered. Experience has given me little confidence in the maintenance sector of Brazilian technology. Well, I would see what would happen.

Walking back to my room, I happened to encounter two apparent electricians standing at a breaker-box in the corridor near my room. 'So, that's what happened to my air conditioning!', I exclaimed to them in Portuguese.

Yes, that was it, they said. To be sure, they followed me into my room, switched the unit on, and checked it. The Medium fan level didn't work, but Low and High did. Good enough. One electrician said he would send someone around later to check the unit's motor.

And so, problem solved. Service so fast that I didn't

even return from making my complaint before everything was all fixed. These particular Brazilians were positively Germanic.

Recife and Olinda, Pernambuco

Tuesday, March 21. Manaus; in transit, Manaus-Brasília-Recife.

Yesterday, on the van tour of the city, the Barrington lady wanted to tell me the latest news from the United States, which she had picked up by watching CNN on television in the hotel.

"I'm not really interested," I told her frankly. "I came here to get away from all that."

Thinking I may have sounded rude—she was only trying to keep me informed, after all—, I explained myself to her:

"When I travel," I said, "I take my body elsewhere. And when I do that, I don't leave my mind behind. To have my body in one place and my mind somewhere else would make me a distracted, nervous wreck. I might as well stay home.

"As for *the news*, the daily diet of disasters, I can't get concerned about it all. I have to economize my feelings. I can't jump in on other people's grievings every day. It would wear my emotions to a frazzle."

The Barrington lady then told me that a woman who had been with her in a group on a jungle excursion for five days was informed by someone else in the party, a news gossip, that there had been terrible floods in Los Angeles. That was where the woman's daughter lived. Was her daughter drowned?, the woman wondered.

She spent the remaining days of the excursion distracted by worry and anxiety. Looking upon the flooded Amazon basin while thinking of her daughter in flood proved an ordeal.

When the tour group got back to the hotel, the woman rushed to phone her daughter, only to find out that she was safe and dry.

The *paulista* lady—they've recently had floods in São Paulo too—remarked, after I had translated the story for her, that, with the way the TV reported *their* floods, you'd think the whole city and its thirteen million inhabitants were all under water. Why, the flood was just some swollen creek in one small area, she said.

The media coverage of distant disasters is just a low form of entertainment. It is a kind of pornography, one that stirs up anxiety, rather than lust.

* * * * *

Today I leave Amazônia behind for my return to the great bulge of the South American continent into the Atlantic Ocean, the *nordeste* region of Brazil, where, instead of venturing upon new paths, I will be retracing old steps. From here on out my experiences will have something of re-experience in them.

I don't like to travel when I'm not feeling tip-top. But now, added to my 54 tick bites and this cold in head and chest are the rumblings of intestinal, or, rather, colonic, disturbance. (Oh, Ariete, what have you done to me?) Surely, I never thought I'd be a whole month in Brazil without that experience.

It all adds up to minor bother, anyway. My perceptions are sharp, my mind is at the peak of its health, I am brimming with vitality.

At certain moments, I feel like a Zen sage. I am immersed, but I am detached. I am excited, but I maintain equanimity. I experience, but I am an eternal sameness immune to mere experience. I have moments of *satori*, enlightenment in spite of myself. I become a selfless self.

I am attuned to the dimensions of my awareness. What do the stumblings of the body matter? This is ultimate health!

* * * * *

Pernambuco. *Per-nam-bu-co*! How exotic that word sounded in my head when I first began my studies of Brazil!

Pernambuco is the major state of the *nordeste*. Recife, its capital, is the metropolis of the entire region.

Arrived to some immediately favorable impressions of Recife, or at least of its airport.

First, at the baggage pickup, the airport provided free carts for use by the passengers. Just like a supermarket.

As I waited with my cart, what came down the conveyor belt were boxes and boxes of electronic paraphernalia,—televisions, radios, tape players, personal computers, electronic office equipment—Sony, Phillips, Hitachi, Panasonic, the names of the inert passengers. Box after box of electronic junk, passing on carrousel round and round before my sleepy eyes...while I was waiting impatiently for the arrival of my underwear.

A lot of people in Recife were evidently going to get themselves wired into modernity. The plane I picked up in Brasília originated in São Paulo. Maybe prices are cheaper in São Paulo than in Recife.

Travel the earth over, and you'll find electronics as ubiquitous as the human. It struck me as incongruous to see so many people back in Manaus walking around talking into portable cellular telephones. Aren't we sophisticated howler monkeys! As for me, I'd rather keep quiet in the jungle and tune in to the singing of the *uirapurú*.

About the help-yourself carts in the airport:

One thing I don't like about traveling is having so many things done for me all the time. Tourism and hospitality are service businesses, I understand; but I like to do for myself, my manhood depends on that, fervent Transcendentalist that I am. If I can't carry my own bags, I just packed too much stuff and should summarily throw some of it out. I'll put up with a little pampering, but I don't want to turn into the Emperor of China. Also, a fortune in small change gets spent on charges and tips for all the trivial intrusive services inflicted upon the traveler.

Besides the carts, another good thing at Guararapes Airport was the taxi service. There is a taxi cooperative. You go to a counter, tell the clerk where you want to go, she looks up the rate in a chart, you pay her, she issues you a ticket, and you are ushered to an immediately available taxi. Very efficient, stressfree, and aboveboard.

My guidebook informs me that the cooperative is more expensive than the freelancers. Maybe so, but I remember the gypsy operators of Recife, who, unable to make their car payments or afford maintenance, used to post a cardboard sign TAXI in the window and go cruising for customers. You were in for a thrill ride with them, not to mention circuitous routes and haggles over the fare. In my Peace Corps days, I was reckless and blest, but now I'd rather pay the extra money for a secure, straight-line transportation.

My driver was a mature woman, who, like a woman, drove well and cautiously (by Brazilian standards).

Even arriving in Recife at night, as I did, I was not blind to the reality that would be revealed by the glare of tropical sunlight. As we drove past the warehouse district, I looked into the darkness and saw spectres. They were the homeless, including children, living in the streets.

Two children had seated themselves right in the middle of the street, and we almost ran over them! My driver swerved around them, then shook her head. 'Why do they do that?', she wanted to know.

Did the street children of Recife usually lie down in the dark in the middle of the street?, I wondered.

The street children of Brazil. Let those who glibly talk about legalizing prostitution in the United States come here first. For the street children are mostly children of prostitutes and unknown, unknowing, uncaring, disappeared casual males.

We passed a parked truck, its lights on, the street dwellers gathered around it. Someone on the bed of the truck was dispensing things. What was going on?, I asked the taxi driver.

They were giving away bread, soap, other subsistence items, she told me. Who was doing that, some church or charitable organization? 'Oh, no,' she answered. Then, after a thoughtful pause: 'Storekeepers do it. Imagine the charity, for storekeepers to give away their own stock to people who, they know, will never be customers,' she remarked.

Midnight charity. A dole in the darkness. The secretive good works that Jesus of Nazareth recommended.

Wednesday, March 22. Olinda.

Arriving at night in Olinda, the suburb of Recife where I'll be staying, I would necessarily get a dim view of my new lodgings.

I am staying at the Hotel Pousada São Francisco. *Pousada* is a new word for me; I can't remember any place being called that in my first time in Brazil. The word might be a cozy affectation from the old country, something like our own *Ye Olde Inne. O pouso* is the landing of an aircraft; *pousar* means to lodge, to stay, to put. Well, I'm in my *pousada*, landed and lodged, but, vagabond that I am, I won't be staying put.

The Pousada São Francisco is not a place the MENA travel agency in Chicago would have recommended to me. They would prescribe a highrise hotel facing Boa Viagem Beach in Recife, or, if I insisted on Olinda, then the one five-star hotel, which, like the Tropical of Manaus, is not in the town, but removed from it, a shuttle-bus or taxi-ride distance away. But I want to mix with the locals here. (In Amazônia, I mostly wanted to mix with the natural environment.)

There was no need for me to stay at a low-end lodging; that would be carrying my nostalgia too far. I wanted something in the middle. I did some research and came up with the Pousada São Francisco. I had to provide Teresa, my travel agent, with its address so that she could make the reservation for me.

The reception clerk guided me up steps and through dark corridors to my room. When he turned on the dim bulb, I was delighted by what I saw: A narrow room, like a hermit's cell, not a bed but a virtual cot, junk furniture, a bathroom with slapdash plumbing. Just the dose of reminiscence and nostalgia that I wanted.

It was only in this morning's bright sun that I perceived that the *pousada* is a lot better than my first impressions. My room contains a TV mounted high on the wall and an air-conditioner that, although noisy, works fine and is adjustable to my approximate preference. The entire *pousada* is being refurbished—(junk to be discarded litters the hallways)—; it's definitely on the up-and-up, of the two-star class. The *pousada* has a restaurant, bar, and even a swimming pool.

It has been recently repainted, in bright blinding white. They used what looks to me like industrial-grade or marine enamel, its surface hard as steel and shining to resist dirt and scuffing. A paint job to last fifty years.

The *pousada* rises in tiers up an Olinda hillside, a mere block from the beaches on the Atlantic. It is on Rua do Sol. Most appropriately to the name of the street and to the tropical milieu, the *pousada's* loudspeaker blared out the old Beatles tune, "Here Comes the Sun!"

When I had my first buffet breakfast in the open-air dining room, I noticed a sign indicating regular inspections by the health department. An electric fan blew a stiff breeze over the trays of breakfast items, making the flies' approach to landing a turbulent experience.

Stepping outside, I saw that the building right across the street is a psychiatric clinic and insane asylum. Mix with the locals, indeed. The asylum is a grand old Baroque building, newly painted pink and white. Feeling a little blue lately? Come right in! We'll soon have you in-the-pink!

A photogenic insane asylum... No, I'm not talking about Brazil. I'm just referring to the institution across the street from the Pousada São Francisco.

* * * * *

I took two walking excursions today, a morning one to get myself oriented and an afternoon one for photography purposes.

The first served more to disorient, than to orient, me. My original intent was a brief foray to the Olinda tourist office for maps and brochures. I studied the map in the guidebook and thought that I could find my way to the tourist office and back by memorizing the route.

However, as is my nature, I got carried away by my exploratory curiosity. I'll just deviate a street or two to see what I might find, I said to myself.

Olinda is very hilly, with winding streets and dead-end *praças*. I soon found myself wandering round and round and up and down. I had my compass, but what good was it, where it was impossible to follow a straight-line course?

I wound up on a main boulevard, walking, I knew, in the wrong direction, but hoping for an intersection, where I could cut back. Meanwhile, the sun was beating down on me, and my bald head was awash with sweat under my Panama hat. I was wilting fast. I had taken on too much.

If I suffered from the heat, I found one who was enduring torture. I encountered a laborer lugging a broken air-conditioner. He huffed and puffed and sweated with the dead weight of it. Now, there's a way to get yourself overheated in the tropics.

I asked directions from a street vendor and staggered back to the *pousada*. I never did find the tourist office, despite walking the length of the street it was supposed to be on.

After lunch and a *descanso* (*siesta*), I decided upon a more calculated approach. Of course the reception clerk could provide me with a detailed town map; I didn't need to traipse off to the tourist office for that. I chose an afternoon itinerary in the vicinity of the *pousada*.

Ascending the street toward the first church on the itinerary—(that's what an Olinda historical walk is, church-after-church)—, I happened to see some young men up in a huge tree, shaking the limbs to release the ripe fruits. One of them told me that the fruits were olives. They looked like olives, but the tree didn't. There was nothing of the twisted shape, haggard bark, and silver-green leaves of the Mediterranean olive trees I got to know so well.

I recalled that, on one of our Amazon jungle walks, Francisco pointed out to us what he said was an olive tree. "What? That doesn't look like an olive tree to me," the Italian-Canadian remarked skeptically.

Well, Brazil is derivative of Europe in some of its cultivated vegetation, as in some of its population and human culture; but much is different here, too. (Recife has been called *the Venice of Brazil*; I'll have to discuss that later.)

Olinda is notorious for self-styled culture guides who accost pedestrians and solicit them. Many of these guides are teenagers. What kind of service do they provide? They'll point out and tell you: The church is made of stones, the windows are glass, the doors are wood, the gold decoration is gold, the church is dedicated to Saint So-and-So and named after him, and so on. Enlightenment from, and for, an idiot. Still, if they persist, they must be suckering customers, but it seems to me one nuisance-step above mere begging.

I recalled James Joyce's crack about the Romans being like the man who made a living by exhibiting the corpse of his grandmother. At least the Romans can tell you granny's biography.

On seemingly every street, I was approached by the so-called guides offering their worthless services. Two boys even solicited me while I was sitting in a pew. 'I'm praying,' I told them in Portuguese. 'Oh...,' the older boy said, drawing back from me. Then, to his younger accomplice, 'Leave the man alone; he's praying.' And they both withdrew.

Aha!, the perfect technique to get rid of the pests, at least while I'm inside a church, I thought to myself.

In the next church, a teenage girl approached me while I was again seated in a pew, now somewhat overheated and getting irritable. When I said, 'I'm praying,' she answered, 'Oh, that's fine' (as if giving me permission to pray in church); 'I'll meet you outside when you're done.'

When I left the church, I snuck behind her back and escaped down an alley.

Farther on, I suffered another intrusion, but it had its charm. Seated at a table in the *praça* in front of the cathedral of Olinda (an ugly and empty church, by the way), innocently drinking a bottle of *guaraná*, I was boxed in by two strolling minstrels. Being alone, I didn't really need any romantic music to become infatuated with myself. But I had neither finished my drink nor paid for it. I would have to endure.

Strumming their guitars competently, the two men began to improvise verses about me, scrutinizing me carefully and singing about what they saw. They alternated verses without pause. They were wrong several times about my nationality—and I shook my head *No* each time, until they guessed correctly)—, and, because I had several lenses with me, took me for a professional photographer. However, one of the verses they sang went something like this:

'This gentleman has a beard turned gray,
And much of his hair has left him,
But he is not an old man,
No, he's not...'

Of course I was delighted and had to tip them. They went on and on with verses about me, as if I were more interesting to them than I am to myself. I completely understood just a few of their many verses. How I regretted my rustiness in Portuguese this afternoon. And I wished I had had a tape-recorder from the airport carrousel, instead of my camera.

When the minstrels moved on to their next remunerative serenade, I finished my *guaraná*.

The teenage son of the proprietor of the refreshment stand noticed the litter at my feet, plastic cups and papers. He started kicking away at the litter, driving it along the pavement, until it was wedged out of sight between a tree and a wall. There, all cleaned up.

Retracing my steps, I shot several panoramas of Olinda's picturesque rich-green landscape from the heights over the deep-blue Atlantic. From the *praça* of the Jesuit seminary, I took a shot that happened to include young lovers kissing, embracing, and leaning hard into each other. I later saw several others. This was a local hang-out for the make-out, I supposed, the setting conducive to romantic hallucinations. How difficult it must be for the Jesuit seminarian celibates to have to look out their cloister windows upon such scenes every day. The tropics is antithesis to any asceticism.

My afternoon excursion proved not so hot and trying as the morning one, but, on my return to the *pousada*, I took a dip in the swimming pool. The water was a bit warm for my liking, but it was cooler than the air, so it did refresh me.

O linda, oh lovely! I floated in a pool in a paradise of sensual delights.

When I returned to my room, I found my laundry already done. Same-day service, what wonders!

Thursday, March 23. Olinda.

Olinda old and new:

I already know this town. My Peace Corps partner Mark moved here from Penedo, and I would visit him when I was in Recife. I even perpetrated the 1970 *carnaval* in Olinda.

I knew at the time that Olinda was a place of some cultural importance in the history of Brazil. Yet, I can't recall taking any sightseeing strolls or entering a single church here. The Peace Corps didn't issue tourist brochures to volunteers. By the time I got to Olinda, I had been living in Brazil more than a year, so Olinda seemed less culturally special than just familiar. We had Baroque churches and pastel houses on hills back in Penedo.

I don't know whether there was much tourism here in 1970; at least, I don't remember any. I have just read that, in 1980, Olinda was designated a National Monument City by the government of Brazil, then, in 1982, a World Heritage City by UNESCO. Such attention must have been responsible for changing Olinda from a byway hillside community to a tourist destination.

In the 1630s, the Portuguese and the Dutch fought for control of Brazil here. Just up the street from my *pousada* is a platform of a shore-battery, its two rusted cannons pointing toward the sea. They don't look like thcy were capable of hitting a moving target, but they could have produced some horrifying splashes.

. . . As I write this, two jet fighters are streaking over the beaches of Olinda. Ready to repulse any invasion from Suriname?

In response to its acquired special status, Olinda is receiving investments in construction and restoration, my own *pousada* but one instance.

Behind one fence you might see a huge empty building, once magnificent, now a deserted mass of crumbling stone. Next door, however, is its contemporary, newly plastered, brightly painted, and occupied.

The Baroque churches range along a similar continuum, from neglected, derelict, and shut to spiffied and reopened. The church of the Carmo, in a *praça* near my *pousada*, is undergoing internal reconstruction and, besides, having its entire surrounding hill stripped and landscaped. Sturdy little sunburnt laborers dig with pickaxes, haul off old red dirt in wheelbarrows, or scamper across the slope like industrious ants.

There is a lot of work going on in Olinda.

Olinda, like many other quaint and picturesque towns, has its artists' and craftsmen's colony. The practitioners of visual aesthetics work in wood, clay, textiles and various other materials, in plain-view open-air, especially near the cathedral, where the tourists, the potential patrons, congregate. I haven't checked out the local wares yet.

The tourists discover that it's not so easy to find your way around Olinda at first, not only due to the labyrinthine streets, but also because many of the street signs are missing, wrenched off the walls by souvenir hunters. The signs, attractive blue-and-white glazed tiles, are a local craft free for the taking.

Olinda, like much of Brazil, is weak in city services and general salubrity. People put their garbage—(in plastic bags, rather than sealed cans)—on the sidewalks, where, if the dogs don't nose into them and scatter the contents, the town's waste sits in the sun, until the sanitation workers come by in an open truck to collect the bags. But when the truck lurches forward, some bags tumble off the back, returned to their producers. So there is trash everywhere. The local beach, both sand and water, is filthy. Some types of tolerance are not admirable.

Nonetheless, there is a gentrification going on in Olinda. Outside money coming in, the rich of Recife, probably. Olinda is so close to, yet so different from, the big city, that the idea of a second house here has its practicality and allure.

Many houses are separated from the street by a courtyard and a fence of steel bars. You could buy and clean up an old house, decorate it to your taste, and padlock the squalor out. Two dobermans to lunge through the bars at passersby, and it's perfect.

By that process, the town gets better. . . . No, I didn't mean that, for only by an ethic of social responsibility, rather than one of personal aggrandizement and wealth-in-a-fortress, does any community get better.

The outsiders must be driving up the cost of Olinda real estate, anyway—(I doubt a Peace Corps volunteer could afford to live here today)—, and, maybe, driving the locals out of their own houses and town.

With enough money, some adaptability, and an inclination toward the *vida tropical*, you'd find Olinda an idyllic place for a residence. Bright sun (but its intensity moderated by Atlantic breezes), the profusion of flowers, fruits, and greenery, the elevated perspectives all around, the mellow and mustiness of colonial history, the creativity and show of the craftsmen, the dynamic street life, including one of the reputed best *carnavals* in Brazil, the spectacle of it all.... You'd be living in a travelog, the envy of some distant TV-watcher in a cold land, him sitting there sullen, watching Brazil on a color TV, while surrounded by gray damp and chill drizzle.

Oh, by the way, that tourist office I spent all yesterday morning looking for, I found today, moved to an office adjacent to my own *pousada*. How we go running off in all directions, frantically searching for what can really be found right at hand.... Well, I sound like Thoreau in touching on that theme. "Nearer and nearer here." In Olinda, for the time being.

* * * * *

A boy was flying a kite from the edge of a *praça* overlooking a slope. His kite soared at the highest heights, while, at the other end of the tether, the boy was distracted in conversation with a friend.

Olinda is situated on a high hill, and there is always a strong breeze off the Atlantic. What accomplishment was it, then, for the boy to get his kite aloft?

We have our hackneyed similes and idioms to describe the easy task: "Easy as pie", "like shooting fish in a barrel", and so on. I'll replace those with a more original, "It's as easy as flying a kite in Olinda."

So, the easy task. Now, what about a coinage to replace the tired idioms of the difficult task, like "finding a needle in a haystack"? Let's see... "It's as difficult as walking down an Olinda street without being accosted by a would-be guide."

Speaking again of which:

I can't even sit quietly in a pew without the so-called guides pestering me. Even my 'I'm praying' line has worn thin.

I couldn't get a prayer in, if I wanted to. I'm surprised that the priests put up with the invasion of their turf by the hustlers. They should want to draw sinners into the church, not let them be driven out of it. What a lost salvific opportunity.

There I was, seated in a pew, getting into a pious mood, ready to yield myself up to spiritual emotion. I was like an Olinda olive, positively ripe to be harvested into the company of the elect.... And what happened? The priests, in their derelict indifference, let a little son-of-perdition drive me from the sacred shrine, the portal of salvation.

If I am eventually damned, blame a lazy, good-for-nothing Olinda priest who couldn't even discharge the simple duty of gatekeeper. I hope the devil runs a more controlled establishment.

* * * * *

You walk the streets of Brazil, and you see most women (not all of them young) with a babe in arms or a babe in the belly or a babe by the hand or hands, a straggler or two behind, one or two or three or a brood, in all combinations of the above. Children everywhere, more and more of them. To what purpose? To what ultimate result?

What is most disturbing to me about Brazil is its children. The population of children now in Brazil approaches, or perhaps has already surpassed, the population of the whole country when I lived here. All those children... What is to become of them?

Today, I saw a boy, a wisp about seven or eight years old, sucking on a cigarette and strutting down the street looking for trouble. There is your Brazilian of the future.

An old woman in the street admonished me not to carry my camera in the back, where it could be cut from me out-of-sight, but to carry it in front, well protected. She followed me down the street, insisting, until I did as she told me. I thanked her and continued on.

That old woman induced fear in me. Why did she do that, ruining my vacation? She wanted to help, of course. She didn't want anything bad to happen to me. Caution, not carelessness, should be my habit.

What was there to fear? The children. Brazil has millions of children who have grown up without parents or homes, hungry, uneducated, with no prospects, but now with a knife or gun and a craving for narcotics. There is danger all around, danger from the children. Watch your camera. Watch yourself!

This society cannot absorb all these children. Where is the food for them, the medical care, the education, the future jobs? How can they be nurtured and raised to responsible adulthood and citizenship? Why do these children exist at all?

Don't go to the Church with that humane question. *Dona* Carolina wrote that a priest came into the *favela* and preached to the poor women that they shouldn't try to prevent having children, but should have and accept the children that God sends them. *Dona* Carolina responded, most appropriately, 'Easy for him to say! He doesn't have to feed them!' So much for the anticontraceptive doctrine of the Catholic Church.

Brazil glories in the youthfulness of its population and seems oblivious to the longterm consequences. There are child-welfare programs, sure, governmental, religious, or philanthropic; but they reach only a portion of children in need. One provision-truck-in-the-night is a charitable gesture but not a solution.

The media in Brazil are as blind to the really significant as they are in the States. The newspapers concern themselves with the level of the dollar and the political intrigues in Brasília; the television with murders, robberies, and bus crashes, some highlights of soccer games and car races thrown in to provide light relief. They just can't see, or are incapable of facing, the really bad of what's happening here.

Nope! This is Brazil, *o país tropical, abençoado por Deus* ('the tropical country, blessed by God'). Sunshine and palm trees, *samba* and *carnaval*. The whole country is just one big beach party.

Well, there are a few dark clouds on the sunny horizon: The cancer-growth of *favelas*, a level of violence the country never knew before, the narcotics trafficking, the incursion of AIDS upon a nonprophylactic, sexually permissive society. (Statistics on social diseases tell a lot about societal pathology.) And what about the problem of the street children? The police of Rio de Janeiro have taken to shooting street children, as if shooting street rats.

Nonetheless, the Brazilians hypnotize themselves with the myth of the tropical idyll. Brazilians have a sentimental and cultural attachment to their country, but little of what could be described as true patriotism or social responsibility. I have little use for the typical *carioca* or *paulista*, the former with their sensual self-indulgence, the latter with their materialistic one. Brazil is a place and a people; it is not a commonwealth.

Never mind *the population explosion* or the apocalypse of universal ecological catastrophe. The problem in Brazil is these particular children here and now. This is not responsible parenthood or responsive social policy.

Unless there is stabilization of the population and a massive shift of governmental effort and expenditure into child welfare, what is the longterm prospect for Brazil but demographic catastrophe and social disintegration? Again, this society just cannot absorb all these children.

It is the children who will write the epitaph of the mythic idyll of the tropics.

The Americans want to adopt third-world children, rescue them, take them off to the United States for a life in the suburbs. I wish that the Brazilians would adopt their own children. The true advocate of children here must have no children of one's own, but take one in to care for. Given the Brazilian population situation, the most noble form of love for a child is responsible childlessness. I don't see the Brazilians rising to that ideal.

Friday, March 24. Olinda.

One thing that hasn't changed during my long absence is the sloth's pace of the functionaries of the Banco do Brasil.

There were only four customers ahead of me at their *câmbio*, yet it took about an hour for me to get two traveler's checks cashed in the local currency. There I was, waiting, waiting, waiting, in suspense, not so much for getting my hands on the cash, as in dread of my next episode of the diarrheal affliction I picked up as a souvenir of Amazônia.

I remembered the operations of the Banco do Brasil in Penedo, so I didn't get impatient or angry, as uncomfortable as I was. If you are weak on forbearance, Brazil will prove deadly to you.

I happened to strike up a conversation with a young woman in line with me. (The bank, knowing itself, had considerately provided chairs, so that we could sit, rather than stand, in line.)

The young woman was a local, but had lived some years in Switzerland. (Imagine the model of contrasting efficiency she experienced there.) She worked in a hotel in Zurich and now has the same type of job in her hometown, Olinda. She didn't like Brazil anymore, she told me, this plodding waste of time in a bank line one instance of why.

She introduced me to her sister, who was standing by, told me that she liked to socialize with foreigners, and, giving me her phone number, invited me for coffee some time. (This was innocent conversation, I must insist. The Brazilians are overtly friendly and hospitable.) Were it not for my indisposition, I would have accepted her invitation on the spot.

The traveler must decide how much to become immersed, how much to remain detached. You have to choose some mix of joining in and staying back. While in the Peace Corps, I mostly did the former; your typical guided tourist does the latter.

Immersion leads to human sympathy, detachment to critical judgment. Each method offers its insights, but also causes its peculiar blindness. On the one hand, I'd like to be a part of it—once again; but that would be pretending. I'm not a Brazilian, I don't belong here. On the other hand, being a peripatetic judge rendering verdicts left and right,—where's the joy in that? So, I drift back and forth between the methods, now practicing one, now the other.

This traveling alone, however, inclines one toward detachment, and so toward judgment and criticism. The lack of social distractions concentrates attention on observation, reaction, and valuation. When no one talks to me, I have only my own thoughts.

The Brazilians, like the young woman in the Banco do Brasil, do talk to me, so, fortunately, I have been striking a dynamic balance between socialization and reflection, between involvement and distance.

* * * * *

You might think that every Latin American is named either José or Maria. In fact, the Brazilians have an astounding variety of first names. When I first arrived in the country in 1968, I was surprised to be introduced to Sócrates.

For a sample of Brazilian first names, we can pick

up the telephone directory of Recife and do a little browsing. Under *Almeida,* a very common surname, we find, in sequence starting at the beginning of A, the following variety of first names that yield the initials A. A.:

Adriana, Adroaldo, Affonso, Agaci, Agamenon (kinsman of Sócrates?), Agenor, Aguinaldo, Airton, Alaide, Alba, Albanita, Albelena, Alberto, Alcides, Alcimar, Alda, Aldeci, Aldemir, Alexandre, Aliete, Alípio, Aluísio, Alvaro, Alzira, Amara, Amaro...

Moving ahead to C, we pick up at: Clea, Cleide, Cleonilda, Cleto, Cleúdio, Clideno, Clodomir, Clovis, Conceição, Corina, Cremilda, Crisanto, Cristenio...

Under D: Dalva, Danniela, Dantas, Darcilene, Débora, Delmira, Denilson, Diana, Diedja, Digenal, Dilermando, Dinara, and even Diógenes (Sócrates' son).

Reading the Recife phone book aloud is a musical entertainment.

In Brazil, it seems that every euphonious combination of letters has been tried out as a familiar appellation. The Brazilian version of my own name, *Normando,* sounds strange to me, but not to the Brazilians. I found another Normando in the Recife phone book.

As with us, the Brazilians derive many of their names from the Testaments Old and New, but they also dip into Greco-Roman history, the latter part of our own education, but, for some reason, not a well-excavated mine for American first names. Well, I'd never name a daughter of mine Phryne.

I wonder whether these Brazilians can identify the

classical personages who are the sources of their names: Antenor, Augusto, Cesar, Constantino, Creuza, Demócrito, Deocleziano, Djanira, Efigénia, Epaminondas, Euclides, the beautiful Eurídice (popularized by the heroine of *Black Orpheus*), Fábio, Leda (keep her away from swans), Pitágoras (in Brazil not a bean eater but a beans-and-rice eater), Sólon, and on and on to Ulisses.

My imagination stirred, I find suggestions of the enchanting damsels of the Shakespeare comedies. Wouldn't you like to frolic in the forest green with Rosineide or Tatiane or Nicette or Olívia—(come to think of it, Will did have an Olivia)—or Evalise or Eulália?

Some strange derivative first names I found were: Wagner, Rossini, Dinamerico (sounds like the name of a bank), Djardiniere (named after a condiment?), Ebenezer (last name not Scrooge), Elesbão (not a lesbian, I hope), Erasmo (*do Recife*, not of Rotterdam), Expedito (a stamp on an express package?), Fausto (ready to make a deal with the devil), Waldénio (a fellow Transcendentalist!), Walkíria (Wagnerian, again), and Zoroastro (who Spake Thus).

Also: Aurora (our own Dawn), Franklin B[enjamin?] and, contrariwise, Benjamin F[ranklin]. How about naming your new baby girl Bemvinda (Welcome!)? There is a Brazilian in Recife named Cheng Ping, an immigrant I would guess but not assume.

This is not to say that there aren't plenty of Josés and Marias. Those two names are at the core of Christian religion, after all, and Brazil has been a Christian country. (You might even meet a Maria José or a José Maria.)

I have a recording of an amusing folksong of the

nordeste, the title of which is 'The Marias I've Loved'. Most Marias have a compound first name or a middle name derived from the attributes of the Blessed Virgin. The singer inventories all the Marias he has loved and complains, in puns on their Marian attributes, how each Maria proved the unsatisfactory opposite of the beneficent promise of her name. Maria of Help was no help at all, Maria of the Appearance disappeared, Maria of the Pleasures brought him pain, Maria of the Graces disgraced him, and so on.

Shifting our attention from theology back to philosophy, I wonder whether the Sócrates I met was as argumentative as his namesake. And did he find a Brazilian Xanthippe to marry?

What's in a name? In a Brazilian one, letter-music, history and culture, creativity, quirks and fancies.

Why not a different name for every single person who is born, unique as is the individual? Then, at last, we'll have heard the last of José and Maria, Joe and Mary.

* * * * *

As with Brazilian names, so with Brazilian faces. I wish I could get everyone's permission to photograph their faces. What an intriguing portrait gallery I could assemble. In Brazil, it is not only the country, but the people too who are the spectacle.

Whatever your prejudices or opinions regarding race, ethnicity, eugenics, and miscegenation, you don't know the reality of it until you have experienced the population of Brazil. A half-millennium of immigration and uninhibited propagation has produced a thoroughly miscegenated people. This country is a teeming nursery of a single human race.

In my own experience, I have found the Hawaiians, another interracial population, the most beautiful of all peoples. Perhaps Brazil has had too many ingredients in the mix, not all of them thoroughly stirred in yet, to please lovers of loveliness. Brazilian faces are not all beautiful, but they are all interesting.

You might say that, when a single stock interbreeds exclusively, it gradually evolves into a caricature of itself. There is no *perfect type*, because the idea of type itself is defective. The *master race*, as we have found out, is a freak and monster.

Now, it's not accurate to say that the Brazilians are of no race, because, in fact, they are the longterm harvest of several races. Which races were the roots in any particular person is sometimes not easy to discern, even if you stare hard into the faces that pass before you. You see traits, but you cannot see genes.

Accustomed to categorizing by traits, however, you speculate about each Brazilian you meet. That one there, slight in build, small boned, with Lusitanian features of face—the Portuguese rootstock. The driver in Manaus, built solid, heavy-boned, square bronze face—Indian origins. Here in the *nordeste,* where sugarcane agriculture required slaves, you see the faces of Africa, a lightened Africa, however, all around you. If you travel in the south of Brazil, you'll see quasi-Germanic, Italianate, Japanian, and who-knows-what-all else. By the time of the extinction of the human, Brazil will have produced every possible type of face. Meanwhile, you can't say, "That person looks like a Brazilian."

The Brazilians like to describe themselves as *the fifth race*; they don't yet understand that they themselves have made race-thinking obsolete. The Brazilians are not adding another race; they are ending race, and, ultimately, racism. Miscegenation eliminates race.

Brazilian miscegenation is linked to the myth of promiscuous sex. The famous Recife-born ethno-sociologist and historian Gilberto Freyre perpetrated the now stereotype of blackies and whities having at each other all day and all night under the aphrodisiac spell of the tropics. Freyre was a scholarly Boccaccio; his books are the most lubricious social studies texts you'll ever read.

As if interracial sex were somehow sexier than same-race sex, and the weather rouses the hormones. Well, there might be something to the notion of climate as conducive to, or inimical of, sexual interest and activities. Here in Brazil, everybody is half-naked, and so more or less always on provocative display. And no one here wears himself out shoveling snow.

I don't know whether frequency of intercourse is higher in Brazil—(or Polynesia or the Caribbean)—than in Winnipeg, Oslo, or Lhasa. We need some vagabond Kinsey to travel the world with a multilinguistic questionnaire to determine that.

This is an erotically permissive society, certainly. *Carnaval* is, or has become, nothing less than participatory pornography. Whether Brazilian eroticism is to the good or bad of individuals or the society has no glib answer. The eroticism of Brazil is already familiar to me; it neither shocks nor mocks me. I title this book *Tropical Ecstasy* out of experience.

Against the Freyrian myth and the raw reality of Brazilian eroticism, I must counterpoise the human physical affection between people here: Kisses, *abraços* (those warm embraces), loving touches between friends, family members, and especially toward children.

I keep marveling that most of these faces I see every day on this trip did not exist when I lived here twenty-five years ago. It's a new, different population. You can't step into the same river twice, said Heraclitus. With the population burgeoning here, you can't visit the same Brazil twice.

The face of a Brazilian is unrecognizable, because it is an everchanging face.

* * * * *

This afternoon, I browsed the artisans' stalls and displays in the *praça* and along the street in front of the cathedral of Olinda. There were plenty of obscene pranks in the crafts, if you like that sort of stuff. Otherwise, going from stall to stall, I discovered that they were all retailing pretty much the same wares. I didn't find anything to buy.

I decided to attend the vespers service at the Benedictine monastery of São Bento. I had seen enough of empty churches; I wanted to see some life and activity in one.

The guidebook informed me that the service started at 5:30, whereas 6:00 turned out to be the right time. Having arrived early to find the great doors shut, I sat on a stoop in the *praça* in front of São Bento.

Dusk settled upon Olinda. Two old women, also arriving early, shuffled over to the church and waited patiently. Now I could see through open windows the church lit up. When I first got there and saw the shut doors, I thought there might be no public service tonight, but the two local ladies and the lights promised differently.

At last, a monk swung open the doors. The ladies and I entered and took pews near the front. The gold of the Baroque ornamentation of the back wall over the altar shone brilliant in the spotlights. Gold needs light.

A lone bat flitted up and down the nave, through the gauntlets of three hanging sanctuary lamps and around the gold curlicues. An emissary from the devil sent to disrupt the service, perhaps. But when the organist rehearsed some deep resonant liturgical tones, the bat's sensitive hearing was assaulted. It flew down a side corridor and fled the church, exorcised.

At 6:00, the bells in the tower began to peal, calling whoever would come to join the old ladies and myself. About a dozen people would drift in during the service.

The monks filed in, thirty of them. Despite the general aging of the clerical population, which has shut down many ecclesiastical facilities, the Benedictines of São Bento presented a good mix of old, middle-aged, young, and teen novices. The future of the monastery looks secure, unless the sensual temptations of Brazilian erotic culture eventually seduce the virile ones away.

The monk whom I took to be the choirmaster hobbled in on a cane, infirm but in charge. He eased down into a chair.

The monks sat in three rows of five each facing the same across the width of the choir. The organ sounded, and they began the chant attributed to Pope Saint Gregory. Their voices were clear, but not loud, considering their numbers. They sang in Portuguese and in Latin.

At certain recurrent parts of the vespers liturgy, the

monks (except for the infirm choirmaster) all stood up and bowed. We in the pews had to do the same. The standing-up and sitting-back-down occurred frequently, which was a hardship on one of the old ladies, who was frail and stooped; but she struggled up gamely, then glided back down, every required time, though she appeared more infirm than the choirmaster.

The Gregorian chant has something of the desert religions of the Middle East to it. It hearkens back to the Jews and Egyptians and those other ancient cultures that developed an elaborate hieratic ritual. That oriental association was reinforced when one monk brought in an incense burner and placed it on the altar, where the priest added more incense to the pile already smoldering.

And so, another sensory element was added to the ceremonial, aroma joining light and sound. I don't think the incense did the singers' voices much good, however. Even the priest coughed when he withdrew from adding fuel.

I wondered whether the monks, hearing about the phenomenal success of that Gregorian chant recording made in Europe, might not be nurturing their own entrepreneurial ambitions of turning music into money. Indeed, I later noticed a sign on the door of the church offering a recording of their chant; but the marketing and distribution network is lacking in Olinda. Anyway, like Benedictines elsewhere, the monks of São Bento make and sell liqueurs, or so I read in my guidebook, but I found neither monkish bar nor liquor store about the monastery grounds.

The vespers service lasted a half-hour. I hurried back to the *pousada* in the dark, rushing through the threatening drizzle of an incipient storm. ...

After I had already made all the reservations for my trip, I found out that I would be missing, by a week, the famous Passion play given at Nova Jerusalem, not too far from Olinda. I just saw advertisements for it on television. The Passion play of Nova Jerusalem would include, I learned in the promotion, fireworks and a laser light-show. Sounds like they're trying to outdo the Resurrection. Well, if the Passion play is more modern technospectacle than a pageant of pious peasants in their devotions, I don't regret missing it.

Now, in the newspaper, I read that they do indeed describe the Passion play as *espectáculo*. The same company that did the special effects for the Rolling Stones tour of Brazil is working on it.

There is show in religion, certainly, but show should not be all there is to it.

Saturday, March 25. Olinda; Recife.

This morning, I got on the bus and headed into Recife for the day. Saturday, shopping day. I should acquire something tangible on this nostalgia trip. Souvenirs, a tourist obligation.

When I got off the bus, there was a deluge. In a few minutes, torrents flowed briskly down the streets of Recife, the desalted and distilled waters of the Atlantic Ocean quickly filthied.

I thought that I'd first spend a few hours on a tour bus, making the guided rounds of the city. I headed through the rain to EMPETUR, the Pernambuco state tourist office. I had gotten the address from my guidebook.

I walked eight blocks, only to find out that EMPETUR had moved...to Olinda! My guidebook proved stale once again.

Well, I was on Avenida Conde da Boa Vista, the main shopping street of Recife. The rain was letting up, so I thought I'd just do a Pernambucan perambulation, and let it go at that.

Compared to Olinda, there is a lot less of historical interest in Recife, anyway. Olinda used to be the colonial capital, Recife its mere port, until Recife's merchants superseded the sugarcane planter aristocracy of Olinda, first in economic, then in political, power. Today, Recife is a metropolitan dynamo, Olinda a mere museum exhibit.

Unlike Olinda, where I appear conspicuous as an outsider among the locals, it was easy for me to disappear into anonymity among the 1,300,000 in the masses of Recife, many of whom were on Avenida Conde da Boa Vista on a Saturday morning. The larger the mass, the more insignificant the individual.

I bought some camera film and a few cassettes of *nordeste* folk music. Then I drifted across the bridge out to the two islands and the port district.

And there on the corner across the bridge, I spied a place I used to frequent. It was now vacant, abandoned, a crumbling ruin, its shutters blown open, the gutted interior visible through them. The whole building, once a beautiful piece of architecture, a complete wreck.

It was toward the end of my two years in Brazil that, one night, I happened to meet there an American recently arrived in the country. He asked me who I was, and, when I told him, he said, "Are you *Normando do Penedo*?" I told him that I was. His jaw dropped, and he stared hard at me. And so it was that I discovered that I had made my picaresque reputation throughout the *nordeste.* I had become notorious, or renowned, depending upon your values.

What times were had there, one night with more living in it than whole years of my life! The building should be preserved as a national historical landmark. Who will undertake its restoration, before it disintegrates into a mound of rubble on the riverbank?

I stood there on the corner in a stuporous funk, confounded by the ruin wrought by time. And I indulged myself in nostalgia and regret. At least, I myself am not yet such a ruin as my old haunt had become.

Withdrawing from demoralizing reminiscences of my past, I made my way through the outdoor flea market. It offered such an abundance and variety of products and junk as to make Chicago's Maxwell Street in its heyday seem lackluster. But I was less interested in buying anything than in just experiencing the scene.

I found a little luncheonette, where I could get a sandwich and drink, and, on a stool against the tiled wall, escape the jostle and surge of the consuming masses.

Then it was on to the Casa da Cultura of Recife, a huge multiwinged structure, once fortress and prison, the cells of which have been turned into shops where they sell locally made artisan ware.

I had heard about the aggressive sales tactics there; I hoped a shopkeeper wouldn't slam and lock the barred cell door behind me, keeping me in custody until I bought something.

There were more than ninety shops in the cells. How much more interesting to have visited the place when it was full of desperate criminals, instead of pushy merchants. Anyway, I bought a map of Brazil imprinted on leather.

Having logged several meandering miles on the hard stone streets and sidewalks of Recife, hot and tired, a bit anxious about a sudden irruption of my indisposition, I became eager to get back to Olinda and my *pousada.*

Buses whizzed by in all directions, but their stops had no route indications, bus numbers, no information at all. What a chaotic transportation system in Recife, and archaic too, with its electric trolleybuses.

I asked a street vendor for information, found my bus, and was on my way.

I arrived at the *pousada* just as the indisposition did, a disappointment, as I am now in the third day of my self-prescribed treatment. Well, it's a nuisance, not an agony.

I took a refreshing late-afternoon dip in the pool.

* * * * *

Now and then, I find myself placing my hand over my right pants pocket, feeling for my fat wallet. It isn't there.

Back in the States, I always carry a wallet, loaded less with money than with the documentation of my identity and my participation in all the connectedness of our modern world. My wallet is bulging with cards of all sorts. From my memory, they are:

* Illinois driver's license
* Illinois auto insurance identification card
* motor club card
* autolube discount card
* VISA credit card
* bank ATM card
* phone credit card
* health insurance identification card
* Berlitz address and phone number card
* membership card in a fraternal order
* Westmont public library card
* Chicago public library card
* supermarket preferred customer card
* business card of one or another salesman I've talked to recently
* calendar card of the current year

Added to the cards are some cash, a blank check or two, fishing licenses, family photos, a lock of blonde hair sealed in plastic.

An archeologist of the future, finding my wallet, could learn a lot more about me than even my books reveal. Now, there's an idea. Instead of wasting those six months writing my autobiography, I should have just photocopied the contents of my wallet.

Well, you might say, a wallet has more in it of the currently useful than the autobiographically significant. Still, archeologists are good at inference.

While here in Brazil, I have left the bulging wallet and most of its contents behind. But the tropics are not the state-of-Nature. I can't walk around here naked, either of clothes or of social documentation.

I, as a foreigner, have to have my passport and that identification card I filled out back in Manaus. As an adventurer in a risky clime, my WHO folder with record of my immunizations. And, as an inevitable consumer wherever I go, my VISA card, traveler's checks, and cash in bills and coins. Brazil is no more an honest land than elsewhere, so I carry keys, to my hotel room and my luggage.

Who are we without our cards? I laugh at the Japanese, who are virtual beasts of burden for business cards. Newlywed Japanese won't even climb into bed together without a ritual exchange, not of vows and bows, but of business cards.

We moderns need a consolidation of our cards. Perhaps some UPC code imprinted onto our foreheads, to be scanned for all purposes. Somehow or other, we've got to get rid of these bulging wallets before our pants fall down.

Sunday, March 26. Olinda; then on to Maceió.

For my Sunday morning excursion, I thought I would visit a few nearby churches, where I should find the locals at their religious observances.

Seeing some people making their way to the beach, I deviated from my intended itinerary and followed them. The church of the sun-worshippers was well attended this hot and sunny day. I saw few there, however, who needed the heavenly graces of a sacramental tanning. They all appeared to be the elect of the sun-god.

As I stood observing, a young man offered me the use of his vacant beach chair. I thanked him for his sandy hospitality but did not avail myself of it. We northland sinners cannot take our solar baptism by total immersion.

Then, on to the churches. I noticed that the doors of the Carmo, which has been undergoing restoration, as I mentioned, stood open for the first time this week. My opportunity to check out the interior.

As I walked ahead, my gaze directed up to the church on the crest of the hill, I took two solid steps into mud left by the landscaping work I had observed all week. Red squishy mud up to my ankles. My Bass shoes went swimming.

I backed off. Looking around, I regretted the lack of a nearby *chafariz* (public spigot) at which I could cleanse my shoes. We set our sight upon a high idealism, only to let the muck beneath our feet mire us down.

Scraping my shoes in the grass as best I could and

nothing daunted, I ascended the bare hill and went into the church. Much of its Baroque ornamentation had been stripped for piece-by-piece restoration; I could see the socket holes in the wall, where the ornamentation had been. All was covered with red-soil dust.

I wandered into the side chapels. In one, I found a glass coffin with the corpse of a white-clad virgin. There was no identification, except an old photo of a girl seated demurely on a bench; her face had faded into unrecognizability.

I found a note, evidently written by a schoolgirl, left on the altar in front of the saintly maiden. The note read, 'Our Lady of a Good Death, please help me pass my exams in school.' (Of course, we all want a peaceful death eventually, but first things first.)

A priest started Mass for a dozen women, so I withdrew.

On to São Pedro, another church I now found open for the first time this week. Mass was just finishing, and the families were streaming out.

No dour piety put any restraints on their behavior. They laughed and sang and threw their babies up into the air. As if Sunday Mass were a memorable occasion, they photographed or videoed one another, even inside the church itself.

At the foot of the steps, the ice-cream vendor rang his bell and loudly proclaimed his available flavors. One woman, after watering the baby, threw the plastic bottle onto the church steps. It rolled, bump, bump, bump, to the bottom. (The bottle, not the baby.)

I went inside and sat in a pew. A girl was singing

hymns *a capella*, her voice beautiful, but spoiled by the loudspeakers, which were at full volume and crackling out distortion.

A few families still socialized in the doorway, and I was in my pew studying the decoration of the nave, when the lights were abruptly extinguished.

An old lady in black appeared, said 'We're closing,' and pushed everybody out with the shutting of the great doors. The ceremonial over, a summary dismissal.

The sun-worshippers, I know, lingered long in their devotions. Theirs is a fervent idolatry. As for me, I retreated to the *pousada* to wash the mud of the Carmo from my shoes.

* * * * *

Hoping that my intestinal affliction was in enough remission to permit sociability, I thought that I would accept the open invitation to visit, and have a cup of coffee with, the young woman I had talked to in the waiting line of the Banco do Brasil on Friday.

I telephoned her several times, but no answer. Out to church, perhaps.

I had noticed a woman guest around the *pousada* the past few days, a foreigner obviously, a German apparently. She had shown no particular overt friendliness. For my part, involved in my writing as I have been, I had not approached her. Seeing her on the veranda today, however, and craving some socializing, I made bold to greet her.

She turned out to be no German but an American from Tacoma. She took me for a Frenchman, she said.

(She meant nothing mean by that, I give her the benefit of the doubt.)

She was a fundraiser for the American Friends Service Committee (but not a Quaker herself). She was here in Brazil to experience firsthand her organization's efforts at grassroots mobilization of the masses. Empowerment is the theme of their missionary program.

She had been to São Paulo and also to João Pessoa, Paraíba, here in the *nordeste*. This was her first trip to Brazil. She was one of those who think that their knowledge of French would substitute for Portuguese, but it wasn't quite working. French would do her better on the next stop of her itinerary, Haiti, God help her.

We sat down to lunch together, and I told her about my own experience of Brazil, mostly dated information necessarily. I'm not really current on the problems and prospects of Brazil, except for what I have observed these past dozen days. Before that, there has been a huge gap in my experience of, and concentration upon, Brazil.

She wanted to know about the Catholic Church in Brazil. I was surprised and pleased to find out from the waitress that *Dom* Helder Câmara, the archbishop of Recife and Olinda in my time, was still alive and active, although shriveled and feeble. In the 1960s, *Dom* Helder was, because of his advocacy of the poor, reviled as a Communist by the military regime, turned into a nonperson, and, although he was too controversial to be made a cardinal by any pope, set on the course to become a living saint instead. The waitress became misty-eyed when she spoke about *Dom* Helder, expressing the same reverence and affection for him that I remember from Maria Heléna.

The fundraiser and I then discussed the inroads being made by *crentes*, the Evangelicals, Pentecostals, and other Protestant sects in Brazil. The titanic ideological battle of the Churches for the souls of the poor!

We proceeded to talk about various other aspects of the Brazilian scene. Our conversation took an analytic, critical course; we became diagnosticians. It is interesting how, when two foreigners get together, they straightaway start to exchange their criticisms of their surroundings, reverting to distance, giving vent to censorious judgmentalism.

I must not associate too much with foreigners while I am here. What sympathetic insights might I have gained today, had Mariane been home to answer her phone.

* * * * *

I'm not sure that airplanes are the most efficient means of transportation between the coastal capital cities of the states of Brazil.

From Recife to Maceió is 160 miles. By the time you commute to the airport, do an early check-in, wait around, take the flight (often late), wait for the baggage at the other end, then take the taxi to your hotel, you might as well take the intercity bus and take in some local color on the way.

Higher technology can sometimes be just so much more rigamarole to old inefficiencies.

Tonight's flight took off from Recife at the exact minute it had been scheduled to land in Maceió.

Maceió, Alagoas

Monday, March 27. Maceió.

You wouldn't think that laundry would be much of a concern in the tropics. So much less worn, so much less to wash? Not so. The perspiration induced by the climate plus the general dirtiness of the peopled environment make frequent laundering a necessity. Brazil isn't Eden.

Speaking of Eden:

The curse put upon Eve for the Original Sin was not only to bear children in labor, but to have to get right up, as soon as Abel, and get to work washing the accumulated pile of soiled fig leaves.

All the rest of her Godforsaken life, Eve had to do the laundry, a task she never had while in the bare state-of-grace. And it seemed that, as fast as she washed the leaves, just so fast her wayward husband and squabbling sons dirtied them.

"Cain, sugar, honey," she used to complain, "do you have to leave your leaves strewn all over the holy land? You make the place look like hell...or autumn."

Every week, it was up-and-Adam again. Damn-laundry-all-the-time was the worst consequence of Paradise Lost. How Eve longed for the good old unclothed days! Now, after the realization of *naked and ashamed*, the whole family was clothed with guilt. Spotless no longer; but could they be, at least, spotfree? That was Eve's grim challenge.

Guilt and dirt were the two words that now described the human race, psychologically and physically. Eve, once the forest nymph, had become a mere domestic drudge. Still indispensable, however, for her husband

and sons had discovered *machismo*, even though they were Jewish, not Latin. Anyway, they wouldn't help with the laundry at all. They just spent their time eden' and drinkin', a lot of which they spilled upon their clothes.

Eve, once so innocent, had become dirt-minded. Adam, dirty-minded, was always bothering her when the laundry had to be done. Lust and laundry just did not go together. How could Eve deter gents? If she couldn't, she would be the one stuck with more childbearing and more laundry.

Some of it was her own fault, Eve admitted. Why couldn't she leaf well enough alone? Apples! *Tree of the knowledge of good and evil*, indeed! All she had now was the knowledge of dirty and clean. ...

Laundry, I have found out, can be one of the most costly items on a tourist's expense account. In my Maceió hotel's laundry service, pants are about $3.00 each to wash, shirts likewise (even if short-sleeved; no discount for that), shorts $2.00, T-shirts $1.50, underwear $1.00 apiece, socks 75¢ a pair, which is 37-1/2¢ a sock.

In Manaus and Olinda, trying to practice my usual Transcendentalist self-reliance and economy, I had searched, in vain, for a laundromat. In the former city, I had to pay nearly $25, and that to wash just enough to tide me over for a few days. Arriving here in Maceió, I calculated that I had accumulated, at the hotel laundry rate, more than $55 worth of dirty clothes.

During my orientation walk after breakfast, I discovered a laundromat about five blocks from the hotel. Off I went, a sack over my shoulder, as in my bachelor days. An hour-and-a-half of reading some Brazilian magazines, and the laundry was accomplished. At almost exactly ten percent of the hotel service price.

For once, a tourist cleans up!

* * * * *

The people of the state of Alagoas are users of toothpicks. After every meal, they grab for one, even if the meal was mush.

They have a characteristic way of using a toothpick. Taking the toothpick between thumb and the closed four fingers, they draw it up to the mouth. Then they put the other hand over the top of the first, fingers together and parallel to the ground.

The purpose of this two-handed, ten-fingered, technique is to cover up an indelicate procedure that might be offensive to observing diners.

When I walk into a restaurant and observe so many diners, their meal finished, with both hands at their lips, it seems to me that an orchestra of harmonica players is about to burst into performance. But no sound do I hear, except an occasional little sucking slurp.

* * * * *

I took a taxi tour of Maceió this afternoon, and it seemed as if I have been away not a quarter-century but a half-century.

The first thing to consider is that this is Alagoas, the state that once had the reputation in Brazil that Mississippi has in the United States, that is, if not at the bottom in any particular category of estimation, then somewhere near the bottom.

Maceió was that "sleepy little village", as travel literature describes the type. Sleepy little mosquito-infested hoveltown in a swamp was more like it. As an Alagoas Peace Corps volunteer, I was glad that I was assigned to Penedo, rather than to Maceió. There were more wholesome surroundings in Penedo, a more attractive urban landscape, a higher culture.

As was the case in Manaus, Recife, and Olinda, I arrived in Maceió in the dark. The revelation of the reality would have to wait 'til the dawn.

From the tenth-floor open-air dining room of my hotel, I heard, at breakfast, the call of the cock of the neighborhood, and I looked down to see a tired horse, under the direction of a slumped peasant, pulling a ramshackle two-wheeled cart. That was Maceió as I remembered it.

But, then, surveying the panorama, I saw mile after mile of developed beaches fronted by highrise hotels one after another. Surely, this is not Maceió; it must be Daytona Beach.

On my tour, the driver told me that, a few years ago, Maceió was used as a locale for the filming of a popular TV soap opera. Because of that, the whole country discovered Maceió as a tourist destination. Not only Brazilians, but foreigners too. By some means I could never guess if I tried, Maceió has become a resort of choice for the Argentines. Might I rendezvous with Isabel Sarli here?

—Oh, Isabel Sarli, if only you had spoken to me in Brazilian Portuguese instead of that Argentine Spanish of yours, what intimacy we might have proceeded to!—

The driver made sure to tell me the names of every one of the hotels we passed. Apparently, the tourist hotels are now the local sights, and, really, the tourists become the local populace. Meanwhile, the place as it was and the indigenous people recede into the background of the scene. The authentic withdraws to the periphery, as the tourists spectate one another in the alien environment they have had constructed for them. That's tourism for you.

Maceió now has 800,000 people, my driver told me; I estimate that at five times the population while I was here before. Maceió has not augmented to its own ruin, like São Paulo or Rio de Janeiro. The Maceióans are industrious, as I could see during the two hours of my taxi tour. There is a mercantile Maceió, as well as a touristic Maceió.

The city is even quite clean, compared to Recife or Olinda. (We're talking narrow distinctions here.) What a wholesome lunch I enjoyed today, in a little self-service cabana near my hotel. The roof was primitive thatch, but the floors and walls were of clean white tiles. Tables and chairs clean. Food appetizing and flyfree. And cheap too.

Alagoas has a joint venture with Pernambuco to develop the beaches adjoining the borders of the two states into a great Costa Dourada, a Gold Coast. The concept is to reproduce the prosperous beach communities of the Florida coast.

Maceió itself has been spending a lot developing the tourist infrastructure. The city beaches are models of attractiveness. There is a walkway running the length of the beaches, *barracas* (restaurant/bar cabanas) at intervals, white sand and clean waters, the glare of the sun reduced by the many *coqueiros* (coconut palms), the characteristic tree of the Alagoas coast.

The *jangadas*, the traditional sailboats of the region, no longer go in search of fish, my driver told me. They now conduct tourists on excursions. Fish have to be pursued, after all, and catching them is no sure thing; but the tourists clamor to get into the boat, so the prospects for the future are more tourists than fish. In fulfillment of the gospel prophecy, the *jangadeiros* have become fishers of men.

I shouldn't take my earlier Daytona analogy too far, however. What is lacking in Maceió is training of those who will serve the tourists.

Last night, the waiter in the bar stood stupidly behind me, until I had to call him over so I could order. He served me a juicy, greasy sandwich, but no napkin.

When, this morning, I asked a clerk in reception where I could exchange currency, he sent me down to another hotel, which, I discovered, did not change currency.

After that wild-goose chase, I found a branch of the Banco de Alagoas (the state bank) just one block from my hotel. They would change cash (at a submarket rate) but not traveler's checks. Keeping the tourist from money to spend is no way to promote a tourism economy.

The reception clerk—the same one who had sent me looking for a *câmbio* where there was none—told me that if I wanted to take the city tour by taxi, I should have him arrange it in advance. So I did. When I arrived at the scheduled time, the clerk gave me a blank look. He hadn't arranged anything. Then I had to sit around the lobby, as someone ran off to fetch me a driver.

My tour driver told me the names of everything—all those hotels—, but did not provide much local color. He was no Francisco of the *Amazon Clipper.* Just a taxi driver, not a guide, really. I did prevail upon him to drop me off briefly at the downtown Banco do Brasil, where, fighting the crowds, I could—at last—get some local cash.

So, you see, Maceió lacks the training programs and service tradition that make tourism work. However, in that, as my driver told me, tourism has been going on in Maceió only since about 1980—(indeed, I remember none in my time)—, a tourist service culture may still develop here.

Anyway, I had no idea that I would find in Maceió what I have found here. I had meant this stop to be just an on-the-way interval between Olinda and Penedo. What a happy surprise. It is heartening to find places one has known getting better and a people formerly poor now making a decent living.

. . . Tonight is the halfway point of my nostalgia trip. So far, so very good!

Tuesday, March 28. Maceió.

There are still fishermen in Alagoas. As I walked the series of beaches northward from my hotel on Pajuçara Beach, at an hour when the sun was risen but not yet high enough to fill the beaches with bathers, I found a few fishermen practicing their ancient trade.

I first saw a practitioner of the throw net. That is a circular net weighted along its circumference. The fisherman wades the shallows, and, when he spots some small dark forms in the water, he slings the net into the air, hoping to capture the fish within the net when it abruptly parachutes around them. Lifting up the net draws the weights together and entraps the fish in the mesh.

That is the same technique I saw used in Hawaii. Success with it depends on sharp eyes and clear water. I watched the portly fisherman—for he had a big belly to fill—make his casts. He caught just a few small fish, which his partner removed from the net and dropped into a basket.

Besides those two, there was a crew of shore fishermen working the beach. They had set out a long hanging net in a great loop, to corral the fish. Three of them pulled in the rope at one end of the net, gradually reducing the loop and drawing in the fish toward the shore. The men walked backwards up the beach, pulling the rope, the highest man then switching to the lowest, rotating their positions, working slowly but relentlessly. At times, one man would leave the one-way tug-of-war and pile the accumulated rope in a neat circle. I could see the floats of the net approaching the shore closer and closer.

The fishermen's work drew a crowd of bystanders,

interested in seeing what the catch would be. At last, the crew pulled the net onto the sand. A mass of shanghaied fish wriggled and flopped about, dismayed at the sudden loss of their aqueous ambience.

The fishermen bent over their catch and began to toss the fish into a big wicker basket. They culled their catch, flinging aside undesirable or inedible fish, like puffers, along with the small crabs entangled in the mesh. The puffer one fisherman called 'a ping-pong ball', but he kicked it into the air like a soccer ball. Some children chased after it.

One boy, finding a crab, pressed it into the sand by stepping on it with his bare foot, tore out both its pincers, then took the crippled crab away with him.

Some bystanders, seeing the rejected little fish struggling in asphyxiated desperation in the sand, picked them up and released them back into the Atlantic. One leathery skinned old lady was especially diligent in her rescue mission. Sunbathing tourists have cash to buy their lunch; they have no need of fish. Whether they tried to save the lives of the castoff fish out of compassion or conservation, I was gladdened to see them do it.

The toddlers and tykes were excited and delighted to witness the catch. They wanted to pick up and examine every little flip-flopping fishy life-form, even as their mothers warned, 'Watch out, it'll bite you.'

One fisherman found a plastic cup, filled it with seawater, inhabited it with a tiny angelfish, and gave it to a small boy, who took the cup and drew it up close under his staring eyes.

An older boy—the same who had mutilated the

crab—filled a yellow plastic pail with all the fish he could grab up. He had put seawater into the pail, but, crowded as the fish were, and because the boy wanted to pick out and examine every individual in his collection, the fish were soon dying or dead, one after another, killed by suffocation and shock and the boy's touch.

I continued my stroll up to the farther beaches, where I photographed and observed and lingered. When I got back to Pajuçara Beach an hour or so later, I saw the same fishermen, the same scene, some same and some new bystanders.

There were two baskets of fish now. In one, a still heap, the gills of the fish flared from their last inhalation. In the other basket, a struggle, twitches, a few feeble flips. And, from the bottom of the basket, now and then a shudder that welled up to the top of the heap.

* * * * *

The beachfront avenue just north of my hotel is the Avenida Senador Robert Kennedy.

I found the name appropriate to my experience of Maceió.

For, it was just after I arrived in Maceió the very first time, in the spring of '68, for my Peace Corps training, that Robert Kennedy was assassinated.

* * * * *

I saw a boy pulling a cart loaded with folding aluminum-and-nylon beach loungers. He stopped the cart, pulled out the loungers, and began setting them up on the beach facing the sea.

Did he rent the loungers?, I asked him. Yes, he did. 'How much?' 'One *real*' (about a dollar). 'For how long?' 'Oh, as long as you want.' 'How's business these days?' «*Fraco.*» ('poor'). 'Well, *carnaval* has passed' I remarked. 'Do you want to rent a lounger?', he asked me in a hopeful tone. 'Not now, maybe later.'

That boy is not in school on a schoolday, let's note that first. Nonetheless, he himself is no lounger. He is enterprising and engaged in a constructive activity. Is education affordable, when a living must be made?

* * * * *

The *polícia militar* maintain a conspicuous presence throughout Brazil. They are stationed not only where one would expect them, as near banks and businesses, where the money is, but also where one would not expect a police presence, as in the doorways of churches. They have their posts in little gray cabins, or they walk the beat in twos or threes, or they cruise in cars, or, in the parks and on the beaches, on a mounted patrol.

Polícia militar: The two words go together, have long gone together, in Latin America. The police are military, the military are police. I'm not talking about MPs. The *polícia militar* is the regular police of the state.

In the past in Brazil, as under other Latin American regimes, the police have been the agents of repression of the people, as much as they have been guardians of law and order and trackers of malefactors. When I lived in Brazil in the late Sixties, I would hear tell of radical university students just disappearing. Brazil is an open democracy today, true, but memories linger. It will be a long time before Brazil has an Officer Friendly.

The officers of the *polícia militar* are outfitted and armed like commandoes. They are all in athletic shape, combat readiness as it were. On this police force, no potbellied sergeant who lives just down the street and kibitzes with the grocers. Stern and noncommunicative, the officers are meant to be a deterrent. If I may venture to judge by mere appearances, they seem successful. But what is deterrence, what intimidation?

There are females in the *polícia militar*, but you wouldn't think them of the same origins as the *moçinhas* who swing and sway their bare-bottomed way down the beaches. It is only the roughest of difference in body silhouette that distinguishes the female from the male officers.

Unlike Rio de Janeiro and São Paulo, Maceió has a reputation for security and law-abidingness. I myself have seen no rowdiness, public drunkenness, altercations, or even raised tempers yet (except my own, when the Banco de Alagoas wouldn't cash my traveler's checks).

This reputation for safety and peacefulness in Maceió is being used by the state tourism promotion agency to draw tourists away from the glamorous but dangerous cities of the Southeast. Strange how Alagoas, which, because of a notorious outlaw of sixty years ago named Lampião, had an image of violence (like the Chicago of Al Capone) has now been transmuted into the opposite myth.

Who are you really safe with? Only the people you know. Tourists attract pickpockets, con-artists, hustlers, shakedown men, and strong-arm robbers. If tourists flock to Maceió, won't all the parasites, hangers-on, and predators be in their wake? Will the time come when the locals yearn for the peacefulness of a simpler day, when everybody was poor but, knowing one another and having nothing worth taking, felt secure?

Anyway, for now Maceió seems free of aggression. So different from Olinda, where I felt besieged, even if only by pests, every time I stepped out.

Maceió is mellow.

* * * * *

I've been thinking a lot about *dona* Carolina lately; I can't get her out of my mind. Strange that, despite all the differences in our respective backgrounds and lives, I feel such a strong kinship with her. It must be the affinity of our mutual self-identification as a writer. And I feel closer to *dona* Carolina than to most any other writer I have read.

What happened to her? I had to find out. *Child of the Dark* was published to literary and financial success. I knew that *dona* Carolina had attempted other works, romantic fantasies, but those were adjudged childish and unpublishable. It was only for the raw reality of her experience of poverty that *dona* Carolina held any interest to Brazilian book readers.

So, she cashed her royalty checks and moved out of the *favela*. But what was her ultimate fate?

I have done some research and found the answer to that question.

Dona Carolina set herself up in a brick house and attempted to live the life of the economically secure. But the money she made somehow slipped out of her hands—(spent foolishly? given away?). Also, the amounts of the royalty checks gradually diminished, as enthusiasm for her book was replaced by enthusiasm for newly published books.

Dona Carolina had no discipline of saving. How could she, having lived on near nothing for so long? You cannot put away any portion of nothing. She soon found herself in arrears on the mortgage, then foreclosed upon, then evicted.

And so, *dona* Carolina returned to the *favela.* (I don't know whether it was the same one in São Paulo where she had lived before and was now hated and resented.) Anyway, she sank back into her old poverty. Her brief windfall of literary riches must have seemed to her just one of her own romantic fantasies.

Just as her book changed nothing regarding poverty in Brazil, so it changed nothing of her own fate. 'We have only one way to be born but many ways to die' was one of her sayings. *Dona* Carolina's way-to-die, like the way-to-live of most of her life, was the worst of all possible ways. She wound up in a pauper's grave.

The writer means nothing to anyone, least of all to oneself, as admitted in a despondent hour. The writer doesn't live life away, but writes it away.

I wonder whether, when she returned to the *favela*, *dona* Carolina also returned to her writing. Are there somewhere, scattered among the heaped debris of the *favela*, further sheets of scrap paper, scribbled on by one who was still, desperately, trying to exert some control over her life...even as it approached its destined end?

Wednesday, March 29. Maceió.

Continuing on the subject of the future of tourism in Maceió: Maceió, *o paraíso das águas* ('the paradise of waters').

I find that I happen to be in town at the same time that the Brazilian National Tourism Mart convention is being held here. Two thousand participants representing 350 tourist agencies from around the world have come to Maceió for the event. It is a golden opportunity for the city to showcase its attractions and advance to the forefront of—(can I say it?)—world tourist destinations. I still can't get over it all.

At 8:00 this morning, BNTM conventioneers had on their itinerary the same activity I had planned for my own, that is, the *jangada* excursion out to the *piscina natural* (the natural pool in the reefs), a mile-and-a-half off shore. I read in my guidebook that, a few years ago, the *jangada* excursion of Maceió was rated by a Brazilian travel industry association as the number-one tourist adventure in the whole country.

The *jangada* is the traditional sailboat of the Atlantic littoral, lagoons, and rivers of the *nordeste*. Its primitive form was tree trunks lashed together as a raft and outfitted with a sail. Today's *jangadas* are still rectangular, with a flat bottom, equipped with a dagger board and single sail fore. The rudder is an enlarged oar, that, twisted at the stern, can be used to propel the craft. The *jangada* is no swift yacht, but it is stable and comfortable. Created primarily as a fishing vessel, now, in Maceió, the *jangadas*—nearly 200 of them—carry tourists on excursions.

I had no idea what would be the best time of day to embark, but a young man named Cícero—renowned authority!—told me that 8:30 A.M. was low tide. The *piscina natural* would be shallow then, a good time to go.

A rain blew in while I was having breakfast, almost discouraging my venture today, but, after dropping their showers, the rain clouds moved off.

Down to the beach I went. The launching point for the excursion happened to be located, most conveniently, on Pajuçara Beach, right in front of my hotel.

I was beckoned to a *jangada* by a well-tanned and vigorous old *jangadeiro*. I waited about fifteen minutes, while he combed the beach, recruiting the six other people to make a boatload.

My *jangadeiro* must have been a senior member of the captain's brotherhood, for he strutted the shoreline with a swagger and air. While soliciting prospective passengers, he carried on a cheerful conversation with himself.

I was joined by three couples. First, two old Japanese. They were São Paulo Japanese, not Tokyo Japanese, as I found out when the Portuguese began to flow from them. The *jangadeiro* asked whether they had any relatives in Japan. Not that they knew of, they shrugged. Brazilians don't bother with any ancestor cult.

Then there was a young couple from Belo Horizonte. They both were on the quiet side, for Brazilians. The girl plumped up her bathing suit well.

The third couple were from Brasília, which I wondered about. The girl had that tiny stature, little triangular face, and narrow eyes I had seen in some *nordestinos.* Sure enough, she was originally from Piaui. She was a happy, laughing, girlish little thing, homely but very charming. She found childish delight in every aspect of the nautical procedure.

The full complement having been acquired, we were ready to set off. The *jangada* was pushed on wooden rollers down the sand and into the water. We passengers waded out and got aboard.

The early morning wind was weak, so the *jangadeiro,* whose name was Rodolfo, had to use the rudder as an oar. He pried and pushed it against the stern. Little by little, we headed out to open waters.

Rodolfo was not born to the sea, he told me. Raised in Junqueiro, in the interior of Alagoas, he discovered the Atlantic as a young man, spat the dust of the interior out of his mouth, and took up sailing, a profession he has now practiced for thirty years, most of them as a fisherman. Rodolfo has some fish tales to tell—500-pound tuna and such.

In about twenty minutes, we came to some submerged reefs and, between them, sandy-bottomed passageways for the *jangada* to course through. We made our way into the *piscina natural* and anchored upwind. Then we got out and waded in the clear shallows.

Meanwhile, more *jangadas* were arriving, shuttling the BNTM conventioneers and other tourists. Soon a long row of *jangadas* was anchored at the reef. The *jangadeiros* rolled up their sails. And a picnic broke out in the middle of the sea.

Wading waiters carried trays of fish and lobster or delivered beer or soft drinks or the juice of a carved out pineapple. Some jangadas were equipped with barbecues; the scent of grilled fish wafted over us as we waded. Vendors with floating platforms displaying their wares hawked seashells or jewelry or souvenirs.

They had even anchored floating *jangada* models to the bottom. Adults played with those, like children in a bathtub. Some young girls started a game of water volleyball. Snorkelers studied the reefs. Some waded, some swam, some soaked, some just stood and marveled at the scene around them.

I sought out the deeper part of the pool. Although it was only midmorning, the sun was strong, so I kept on my sunglasses and Panama hat, as I breast-stroked my way through the water.

I stood for a while at the edge of the submerged reef, which provided penthouse apartments for the little fish. I put my hand near one tenant. He kept circling my hand and charging it aggressively. "Be off, trespasser!," he warned in body language.

The occasion was more festive than *carnaval.* More wholesome, certainly. Young and old mingled and exchanged appreciative pleasantries. Most of the tourists seemed to be Brazilians from the Southeast. I talked with many of them and tried to understand what I could. My comprehension lags behind my fluency; how hard it is to learn more than we have to say.

I counted fifty *jangadas*, so, figuring six to eight per boat, there must have been more than three hundred people in the *piscina natural.*

At the peak of the gathering a helicopter suddenly appeared, circled us slowly twice, and shot a video of the scene. We all waved to the cameraman. A few minutes later, another helicopter shot its version of the party...part of the BNTM promotion, I would guess.

After two hours of exploring, socializing, feasting, steeping, and enjoying, our little group climbed back aboard the *Baleia Azul* (the Blue Whale, the name of a hotel. Every *jangada* sail bore its colorful advertising.). Actually, the *jangada's* name was *Estrela d'Alva*, Dawn Star; but the name on the sail, commercial as it was, was more conspicuous.

By now, the wind had picked up, so we sped back to land on Pajuçara Beach.

The *jangada* excursion to the *piscina natural* has been my own number-one tourist adventure on this trip. Sure, the Amazon cruise was exciting and fascinating, but this little boat-party in the distant shallows was such a happy combination of Nature and human nature.

* * * * *

I went to the bus station to buy my ticket to Penedo for Friday. (I had gone there yesterday, only to find out that they sell tickets only two days in advance or the day before. My American foresight, just premature timing here.)

The *jangada* excursion having proved a fully satisfying tourist activity for one day, I decided to go downtown for shopping.

Maceió Centro is a bustling area of mercantile enthusiasm. Everyone there was trying to sell something, to make some little contribution to the consumer economy. No pork-belly futures or financial derivatives being traded in downtown Maceió. Instead, they deal in more immediately useful commodities. On the steps of the post office, a boy was selling airmail envelopes, seventeen for fifty *centavos.* (I wondered how he determined his pricing structure, what profit margin he made, what his sales volume was.)

If you are thirsty, a street vendor will offer something to drink; if hungry, something to eat; if overheated, something to cool you off. And every little odd-and-end (*miudeza* in Portuguese) is available from the street vendors.

There are actually two parallel shopping areas in one. The buildings deal mostly with high-priced items, like appliances and electronics, which can pay the overhead, while the transient vendors sell cheap items that generate enough profit income to put food on the table.

I was startled, when a girl walked up to me and sprang open a shoe-box in my face. I recoiled from the throbbing life-forms within. They proved to be kittens that she was trying to sell. She had even made little gold cutout decorations that she placed among the kittens to glamorize the display. Wouldn't I buy one of the kittens? I would help myself, help the kitten, and help the girl too. No, I couldn't transport a kitten back to the United States. We have our own feline overpopulation problem.

Never mind the Latin-American stereotype of the lazy *péon* dozing his life away under a *sombrero* in the hot sun. The people of Maceió are hard workers. Very different from my memories of twenty-five years ago, I have encountered very few beggars with their hands out. No, Maceió is willing to work. These people have a work-culture, even though no Protestant ethic. I wished them well in every little enterprise they have undertaken.

Maceió has advanced from shaky subsistence to economic competence. Perhaps prosperity lies ahead.

In my shopping quest, I did find a cultural treasure, a collection of songs from the half-century career of the great *nordestino* folk singer, Luiz Gonzaga. 33-1/3 r.p.m. records, an old technology for an old-time singer.

As is my wont from my Rome days, I wandered up and down unknown streets to see what I might find. I didn't have my compass with me, and my guidebook map didn't include the names of all the streets I was stumbling over, so I got disoriented.

I logged miles in my aimless meanderings. At last, the great low blue that appeared on the horizon oriented me to the Atlantic, and, so, to the direction of my way back. I found a bus (marked *Vaticano*!?) and returned, footsore, to the hotel.

The welfare of Maceió is improving. Because the people of Maceió have taken their welfare into their own hands.

* * * * *

I had dinner in one of the *barracas* on the beach. The main course was a grilled cross section of some fish that, judging by the girth, which filled the tray, must have been of some imposing bulk as it cruised the Atlantic eating, in the days before its fate today,—hooked, cooked, and eaten.

My affliction now apparently defeated and my medication dispensed with, I could also enjoy my first cold beer in a week. The fish and beer were a fine combination for a dinner on a Maceió beach.

It was quite dark, so, after dinner, I strolled down to

the shore to look at the stars. Behind me some boys sang and danced in the sand, just happy with the place and the warm night.

Approaching the waterline, I stared out into the sky over the south Atlantic. That sky was very black, so the stars shone brightly against it. Just a few clouds drifted in the air, reflecting back the streetlights of Maceió. The salted breeze, as it passed onto the land, left its trace on my lips.

Shielding my eyes from the shore lights, I searched for the *Cruzeiro do Sul*, the Southern Cross, the most prominent constellation of the southern hemisphere. No Big Dipper to be seen in this sky. I am on the flip-side of the globe.

How is it that, although I remember well the lands of Brazil, I retain no memory of the skies? Was all my dreaming of those days mere daydreaming?

Where was that *Cruzeiro do Sul*, orientation point for all navigators of southern waters and wanderers over southern terrain? I didn't know where to look.

There were various groups of stars that, with little necessary pious imagination, could be linked into a cross. But which comprised the true *Cruzeiro*?

I'm not from here. Even though I passed through many times long ago, I don't really know my way around. I am a stranger, not from another planet beyond those stars, but from the invisible lands above the equator, which might as well be the same distance. A northerner, here disoriented.

I need to reorient myself. There is a new heavens here, and, under it, a new earth and a new people. Just when I think all is familiar, I find all strange. I am experienced and well traveled, but, now dislocated, I have become a naive lost wayfarer once again, in awe at the strangeness and differences of it all.

The only way to find your way is to deliberately get yourself lost.

Thursday, March 30. Maceió.

Yesterday, I asked Cícero at the travel agency to set up a tour for me today. I told him I would accept any one of three of his standard itineraries. He promised to phone me later in the day, when he had worked something out.

No phone call came, so, immediately after my usual early breakfast, I walked up the beach to the agency; it's only a couple of blocks.

I found Cícero at his desk, reading the news of the day. Their agency had nothing going, he told me. That's why he hadn't called. It being low season, they couldn't assemble a quota to make it worthwhile to run their buses.

Cícero began to phone other travel agencies to find out what they might have scheduled for the day. Many of the other agents weren't in their offices yet, so Cícero left messages for them to call as soon as they got in.

There happened to be a big poster of the Chicago nightscape on the wall behind Cícero. As we waited, I did a little promotion for Chicago to the travel agent.

After my sitting there a half hour, it became apparent that nothing would turn up. I bid Cícero a good day and left. I remembered a tour hustler who had approached me yesterday on Pajuçara Beach about a schooner cruise of the lagoons. I would try to find him.

He found me, and signed me up. The cruise left at noon, so I could rest the morning. I still felt worn from my shopping trek. A cruise should be relaxing.

A few minutes after noon, I was picked up in a

Volkswagen van and driven to Pontal da Barra. The first activity was, most sensibly considering the time of day, lunch in a lagoonside restaurant. I ordered fish with cooked vegetables and rice.

I sat next to a young couple. He was another Japanese Brazilian from São Paulo. She was tall, fair-skinned, and fleshy. You could almost take her for a Midwest American farmgirl; but, no, she was *paulista* too. They were on their honeymoon, she told me.

They looked none too happy about it. They weren't very communicative, either with each other or toward their fellow tourists. He had a sour look on his face; yet, as I surveyed her warm skin and curves and cleavage, she seemed to offer a paradise of sensual honeymoon delights.

Experience has made me expect the worst of honeymoons, but maybe they just had had too much sun. They had spent the morning on the *jangada* excursion to the *piscina natural*, the bride told me. That's where honeymoons go wrong—too much sight-seeing and miscellaneous activities, to the neglect of the essential task.

Maceió must be somewhat of a honeymoon mecca. When I ran into the Brasília Brazilian and his little Piaui girl again at the artisans' fair last night, they told me that they too were on their honeymoon. That one, at least, seemed to be going well. She was bubbling as usual, and he was in fine spirits. There was a gentle-manly quality about him that I liked.

After lunch, we boarded the schooner—the *Cisne Branco* (the White Swan). I had no sooner sat down than I was ordered to disembark. It seems that each tour hustler worked with a different shipowner. Mine was affiliated with the *Dakkar*, so I had to change schooners.

I liked the looks of the *Dakkar* better; some good, dark, weathered wood on her. I would later regret my transfer, however; for the Swan was a swimmer, the *Dakkar* a floater.

The *Cisne Branco* was off a-sailing, as the *Dakkar* sat dockside. In a while, we pulled out, only to pull in at another restaurant down the shore, where we waited. Then we cast off, only to return to the restaurant where I had eaten. We waited some more, then shuttled back to the other restaurant.

«Este barco sempre chega, nunca vai» ('This boat always arrives, never leaves'), I remarked to a fellow passenger.

It then became apparent why our departure was delayed. Agents in the restaurants were trying to recruit more passengers from among the diners, to make up the *Dakkar's* full capacity of twenty-five. Some diners did come aboard, so, at last, we stopped kissing the shoreline and steamed out, the diesel engine hammering the block with its pistons (if that's the way diesels work; anyway, it was a noisy engine).

Alagoas, the name of the state, derives from *As Lagoas* (The Lagoons). We were on the brackish waters of Mundaú, one of the two principal lagoons of Maceió.

We noticed white jellyfish in the water, great numbers of them, pumping their way by, some being forced to the surface by the turbulence of our wake. The captain brought one aboard and held it in his hand to show us. I was surprised at his handling it, but he said that that kind didn't sting.

He called it *cebola* (onion), and its color was, indeed, like a white onion; but its shape and size were more like a grapefruit. The *cebola* kept its form in the captain's hand, did not collapse and ooze into slime on the deck. He held it like a bowl; it must have been the water in it that made it retain its rotund solidity.

The itinerary of the cruise was called *Nove Ilhas* (the Nine Islands), and it started out well. The captain pointed out the various islands in the lagoon and told about them, although mostly in terms of which industrialist or politician owned which island and what development plans for each had failed or were still in-the-works. As if Nature has no significance without such utilitarian reference points. (I remember the helicopter pilot on Maui pointing out, as we passed over some of the most spectacular sea-cliffs in the world, a recording studio owned by one of the Beatles.)

Some islands in the lagoon had *coqueiros* (the characteristic coconut palm trees), others bore mostly scrub. One island had been raked clean for a *sítio*, the house of which was situated on a point. Another island was occupied by a small fishing community, plying the traditional trade of the Alagoas littoral.

There were fishermen throughout the lagoon. I watched one boy, who had set up a net across the width of a little cove, slap the water with a flat stick to drive the fish into his net. Many were working throw nets, either from boats or while wading in the shallows. I saw quite a few fish jump, so I think the fishermen still enjoy fertile waters.

So far, so good.

The young captain had red hair and that leprechaun-look of an Irishman. I entertained a fantasy that he was the son of some Peace Corps volunteer who had served in Maceió and, on one fateful night, succumbed to a propagative impulse. A moment's reflection, however, dispelled the possibility. For the very last Peace Corps volunteer, no other than myself, had left Alagoas twenty-five years ago. The captain was no son of mine, and, besides, he must have been only twenty or twenty-one.

The variety of physical types of the Brazilians induces all kinds of genealogical speculations. In Brazil, the tree with the most luxuriant foliage is the family tree.

Our captain may have been no Irishman, but he was a drinker. Both he and the mate at the wheel were sucking cans of beer the whole time.

We approached the opening of the lagoon to the Atlantic, where the sea surges in or out with the tides. There was an island there, a sandy dune devoid of trees, its only vegetation some sparse grass and ground vines. The captain announced that we would be making a stop at the island for exploring or swimming. There was a *barraca* bar there; it was a broad, open shelter roofed with palm fronds.

I set off exploring the shore on the seaward side. The waves were clawing away at the sandpiles, and there was a stiff breeze.

Combing the beach, I spied a weathered white hump protruding from the sand. I pulled it out. It turned out to be...the skull of a dog. A salty dog, most certainly.

Farther along the shore, I found his ribs and vertebrae. Had that Fido, a *jangadeiro's* dog, been given a burial-at-sea? I wanted to set the skull on a post, as a taboo-marker, to scare off trespassers upon canine sacred ground, but, after showing the skull to two fellow excursionists, I dropped it back into its sandy grave.

I had a bit of a sunburn from yesterday's *jangada* excursion, so I decided I wouldn't go swimming. Anyway, the rough sea looked dangerous, and the lagoon waters were suspect of schistosomiasis and the cholera that still bedevils Alagoas.

I resorted to the shade of the bar, where I noticed the captain and the mate slumped at a table and drinking beer, emptied bottles already accumulated.

Here was where the excursion bogged down completely. The bar stop dragged on for two hours. I sat there impatient, wanting to be off again cruising, not drinking myself into a stupor in the heat.

And I watched the *Cisne Branco*, which had earlier cruised by us, return. It drew near the island, but not for the bar. It merely used the island as a block against the swift current, then cruised on to new waters. There was the schooner I should have been on, even if I had to put up with the glum looks of honeymooners.

At last, we boarded the *Dakkar* again, only to head straight back to dock. Captain and mate were sucking beers still; they had been at it for four straight hours. I hope the captain owns the boat, for, if I were the owner and found out that he was managing my property while fueling himself nonstop with alcohol, I would promptly tie a rock to his leg and send him to the fate of the salty dog.

So, there was my schooner excursion: One hour in the van, one hour in the restaurant, two hours in the *barraca* bar, and less than two hours cruising. The whole thing seemed like a sweetheart deal among restaurant, boat, and island *barraca* bar.

The tour ended with confusion over the van shuttle and a half-hour wasted sitting in the van at the lagoon, just as the mosquito hour was arriving.

Two Argentines had apparently decided to dawdle over a dinner at the lagoonside restaurant; they thought the van and its other six passengers should just sit awaiting their completion of a dessert and cordial.

There was an extended, pointless argument between our van driver and somebody coordinating the tours over which driver had brought which excursionists. Our driver complained about the disorganization, then, in an upset, drove off with us.

The schooner cruise was supposed to climax in a *pôr-do-sol*, a romantic sunset. There was a *pôr-do-sol*, of course, Nature's timely and reliable one; but I did not see it, because, at the romantic moment, I was inside the van, speeding through the streets of Maceió, where the buildings obstructed all views.

The chubby little brown boy, who had kept up a charming chatter with his father the whole cruise, was now dead away asleep, his head limp on his father's hairy chest.

* * * * *

I had a convenient dinner in the hotel's rooftop restaurant/bar.

Looking up at the dark heavens, I felt a sudden curiosity. I recruited the waiters to help me find the constellation, *Cruzeiro do Sul*. Where I lived, I told them, you can't see the *Cruzeiro*. You can't see any of the stars of Brazil, in fact. These stars were all strangers.

One waiter jumped to the task of helping me find the *Cruzeiro*. The two of us went up the few steps to the level of the swimming pool, from which we could see over the surrounding walls. We were on the tenth floor. No buildings would block our view of the 360-degree panoramic black canopy of the night sky.

The waiter's initial enthusiasm evaporated quickly, as his eyes searched the western sky in vain. It was too cloudy to find the *Cruzeiro*, he complained. There were some clouds about, true, but not so many as to frustrate stargazing, I thought.

The waiter called his colleague to help me, then withdrew. My second culinary astronomer turned off some of the lights in the bar to reduce the earth-glare. *«O Cruzeiro...O Cruzeiro...»*,he repeated, as if looking up a number in a phone book. He started his search in the northeastern sky.

Why was he looking in a direction opposite the one his colleague had searched? The *Cruzeiro* moved around, he informed me; you could find it in different parts of the sky. Pivoted around on an axis, like the Big Dipper of the north, I thought to myself, but not moving around just anywhere. What good would the *Cruzeiro* be for navigation, if it were capricious in its appearance?

The second waiter pointed to a very bright star at the zenith and announced it a component of the *Cruzeiro*. Then, sweeping his arm across the heavens, he told me that the *Cruzeiro* ran 'like that'.

Again, I was doubtful. How could a constellation used for navigation sprawl across the whole visible sky?

By that time, the first waiter had brought my omelet and rice, so I descended from the star-search to eat my dinner while it was hot.

The waiters proved no more competent guides to the stars than the accosting teens that pretended to be guides to the culture of Olinda. Well, I had pressed the waiters to a service they had never advertised. Even though they worked every night in the rooftop restaurant under the open skies, what use to them was stargazing? The *Cruzeiro do Sul* holds no interest to the earthbound, provides no orientation to those whose navigation is from kitchen to cash register.

* * * * *

When I lived on my *sítio* in Penedo, I had in my study a hand-carved wooden model of a *jangada*. The jangada is a symbol of Penedo's river economy, as it is of Maceió's ocean coastal economy. My *jangada* plied no waters, however; it was in dry dock, atop my bookshelves, under the proclamation of my mystical motto, DYNAMIC HARMONY.

Somehow, when I left Brazil, my *jangada* stayed behind. Perhaps it was too bulky and fragile to pack; or perhaps I gave it as a present to João, my ever-present neighbor boy.

This past week in Maceió, I have been searching for another *jangada* model to take home with me. There is an everyday artisans' fair right on Pajuçara Beach in front of my hotel. But the *jangada* models they sell there look as if they were assembled from a kit on some production line. I will never buy a souvenir that says *Souvenir* on it, or, in Portuguese, *Lembrança*.

I mentioned before that there were some floating

model *jangadas* anchored to the sandy bottom of the *piscina natural* when I took the excursion there. That was the kind of *jangada* model I wanted.

Sitting in a Pajuçara Beach bar frequented more by the locals than the tourists, I happened to see two nicely made *jangadas* on a table. They were reminiscent of the roughhewn one I had once owned. I went over to examine them, and I met the man who had made them.

Jorge was a sundark young man, born in Rio de Janeiro, but moved to Maceió when he was a boy. He was a *jangadeiro* himself, owning four of them, all now making the tourist excursion to the *piscina natural.* He made a few models now and then as a sideline and for love of the vehicle of his trade.

Jorge the *jangadeiro* pointed out to me the details of his model, authentic, as only a boat operator knows every dimension and item of his craft; (by *craft*, I mean both the boat and the modelmaking). Jorge's model even had its rollers for launching the *jangada* from the sand, its dipper for wetting the sail, and its little fish basket aboard. After discussing and admiring the model, I bought it for about $20.

Jorge then poured me a beer, and we had a little conversation. I asked him about the advertising printed on the *jangada* sails. All the *jangadeiros* had their advertising contracts, Jorge told me. He himself received the *reais* equivalent of $750 every six months to advertise a liquor. That kind of steady income would pay for the boat, which is, after all, a simple craft with low maintenance.

And wasn't a *jangada* a good medium for the advertisers?, Jorge continued. Their names on the beautiful sails in a beautiful beach setting, all the rich tourists flocking to read the advertising, not to mention the other no-cost appearances on picture postcards, in tourist promotion literature, and, now and then, in a feature on local, or even national, TV.

The *jangada* excursion to the *piscina natural* is the most popular tourist activity in Maceió, so, between the advertising revenue and the excursion fees, a *jangadeiro* can make himself a good living, Jorge said.

We then talked about Maceió. Jorge loved it here. He wanted no part of the crime and terror in the streets of the big cities of the Southeast. He told me that most of the owners of the stalls in the Pajuçara artisans' fair were from other parts of Brazil, taking refuge here, where one could make a living and live in safety.

Jorge attributed the security in Maceió to a shoot-to-kill policy of the law enforcement. The *polícia militar* gunned down eight desperadoes, including a woman, just last month alone, he said. But I argued along the explanatory lines of «*A gente das Alagoas é uma gente boa*», that is, *Alagoanos* are good, decent people.

Well, I had my *lembrança* at last. If I succeed in transporting it safely by land and air, a *jangada* will again sail invisible waters over a bookshelf in my study.

Destino: Penedo, Alagoas

Friday, March 31. Maceió; to Penedo at last.

The Maceió beach, *A Praia dos Sete Coqueiros*, is named after the seven coconut palm trees that are the landmark on its site. As I passed there this morning, I counted five *coqueiros* in a clump, and, nearby, a group of four more. Neither counting just one group nor the two groups added together amounts to the *sete* of the name.

When I took the taxi tour, the driver explained that the assemblage of five were the originals. There were two more in that group, but they had died, which accounts for the discrepancy between the name of the beach and the current reality of the site. Well, I suppose it wouldn't be practical to change the name of the place at every mortality.

As I looked up in admiration at the nine lofty *coqueiros* this morning, a street vendor noticed my interest. We began a coconutty conversation. According to him, the seven *coqueiros* of the name were the five in the one group and two of the four in the other. The remaining two had been planted later. I objected that the four looked of similar age, but he insisted that two of them were smaller and younger. Well, I suppose it wouldn't be practical to change the name of the place at every birth.

The vendor told me that he himself owned a *sítio* that contained eight hundred *coqueiros*. (I wondered why he was selling T-shirts and not coconuts.) Unlike these old-timers—(he estimated their age at eighty to one hundred)—, his *coqueiros* were low to the ground, making easy pickings. Were one to ascend the towering coqueiros we were looking at—and, old as they were, they still bore coconuts at various stages of development—, you would risk death if you fell or if the old tree broke under your added weight.

The coconut palm cares little for the willful verticality of the pine. Instead, it extends itself into the air at any angle, and curves like a snake as it grows. Its fibrous structure keeps it intact in any ocean winds up to hurricane velocity.

As during this trip I have heard Nature discussed in terms of utility, I might as well do so myself. The coconut palm produces that most valuable of commodities in a saltsea environment, namely, fresh water. I bought a chilled coconut from a vendor on the beach and enjoyed its water (not milk, as it is commonly described). I would guess that the cask held about a pint. *Coqueiros* seem to bear irrespective of season, and they bear plentifully.

Besides the fresh water, there is the meat of the matured nut, the inner shell (a perfect bowl), and the fronds, which may be woven into a variety of useful domestic items (baskets, mats, and such) or used whole as tropical roofing.

One of the Maceió beachfront *barracas* was having its roof repaired. That process consisted in merely cutting the weathered palm fronds from the wood frame, pushing them off the roof, and lashing on some new green fronds. Not a durable roof, but a readily available and therefore cheap one. It doesn't have to support the weight of snow; if it leaks some rain, that is of little consequence in a *barraca* bar, where some of the patrons may already be soused. The palm frond roof provides the welcome cool of shade on a hot beach.

While I'm presenting this consumer's guide to

coconuts, I should also include the required safety advisory: “Warning! Never snooze at the base of the coqueiro trunk!” For, if the tree chooses to release a ripe coconut at that time, the hardness of the nut times the distance of fall produces a momentum and impact that would leave little doubt about which nut would be the one to crack. I remember reading in a local paper about just such a fatal accident. I think its headline was ‘From *Descanso* to Eternal Sleep’.

Despite my dire warning on that last point, I conclude that, for both natural aesthetic and utility to humans, the coconut was the best flotsam that ever washed onto a coastal beach.

* * * * *

As I was packing for my trip to Penedo, I received a phone call from a travel agency affiliated with the one that coordinated my trip. The caller offered me air-conditioned limo service to Penedo. Otherwise, how would I possibly get there?

I thanked the caller for his concern over my welfare, but told him that I had already bought a bus ticket.

I didn’t come back to Brazil to stay detached from Brazil. I’m not going to plunge myself into hardship for the fun of it, true, but I want means and avenues of contacts with the people I once lived with and among.

There have been remarkable changes in Maceió’s transportation infrastructure, as in so many other aspects of the local economy. Their new bus station is an open, airy pavilion with a steel and aluminum roof. The station is clean, attractive, and efficiently laid out. A far cry from the filthy Maceió bus station of the past, with its beggars, unsavory characters, and abominable toilet facilities.

The buses too are modern. Somehow, I don't think I'll be sharing this 110-mile ride to Penedo with chickens and pigs, as in the days of yore.

There are certain aspects of local color the passing of which I regret not at all. I'm not nostalgic for squalor.

* * * * *

My departure from Maceió couldn't be expeditious, because hotel check-out time was noon, and I had bought a ticket for the 6:00 P.M. bus. The reception clerk gave me a *tolerançia* until 3:00. That was the best he could do. He didn't own the place.

On the way to the bus station, I got a third explanation for the *Praia dos Sete Coqueiros* problem. The taxi driver who took me said that two of the original *coqueiros* began to look sickly. In anticipation of their demise, the city planted two new ones. But then, to everyone's surprise, the two sick ones recovered, and so now there are nine. Well, I suppose it wouldn't be practical to change the name of the place over a little matter of sickness and recovery.

I had to sit around the bus station for more than two hours. I idled away my time thinking about *coqueiros*.

I have at home a color slide that I took in 1968. It clearly shows, not seven, or nine, *coqueiros* on that beach, but thirteen. What story can I concoct to explain away that even wider discrepancy? Are the *coqueiros* of Alagoas peripatetic? Or are they beach jack-in-the-boxes that now conceal themselves in the sand, now pop out into the air?

My head became crowded with coconuts, and with numbers. The first story I had been told was 7 minus 2 deceased, with 4 others added; the second story, 5 plus 2 makes 7, plus 2 new ones; the third story, 7 minus 2 sick plus 2 stand-ins plus 2 recovered. Now, if I started with the original 7 of the name, subtracted the 2 dead ones of the first story, that makes 5; add the 4 new ones of the first story, makes 9; add the 2 new ones of the second story, makes 11; add the 2 stand-ins of the third story, makes the 13. There, *Sete Coqueiros* problem solved. Might as well leave town now. ...

I was distracted from my coconut considerations—(I was going to do an audit of my accounting)—, when I was approached and engaged in conversation by a young man from Arapiraca, a big town in the interior of Alagoas.

He had come to Maceió to look for work, but, unsuccessful and discouraged, he was on his way home. He stared at, and marveled over, all the baggage I had with me. I explained that I was traveling for a month and needed it all. Then he stared fixedly at me, in that unsettling way that rustics do when they look upon incomprehensible outsiders.

The boy seemed a bit simpleminded. When I told him I was from Chicago, he asked whether there might be work for him there. I told him that he'd have a hard time of it in Chicago, because he didn't speak English. Would it take a long time to learn?, he asked; he'd learn English, if they would give him a job afterwards. Oh, English would take many months to learn, I answered.

The bus pulled into the bay, so I boarded. I had a window seat, the preferred location for fresh air and unimpeded sightseeing. Only a half-dozen passengers boarded with me. What luck! We would speed to Penedo on a mostly empty express.

Not really. The bus stopped in front of the train station, where there waited a mass of people, who transferred aboard, until we were full up, the aisle crowded with standees. The bus was not air-conditioned, so I opened the window for the breeze.

The advantage of night travel in the tropics is that it is cooler, and, there being less traffic, also faster. It was already dark when we left Maceió.

It soon became apparent to me that we were not going to Penedo by the interior route I knew, but by a coastal road that didn't exist in my time. AL-101 is narrow, two-lane, but paved with asphalt and of fairly good surface.

We sped along past the plantations of *coqueiros*—let me think no more upon them!—and sugarcane. And I spotted, at last, what I believed was the *Cruzeiro do Sul.* It is just four stars in a trapezoid, more kite than cross. There was no moon, so the stars were especially bright.

I thought that I had bought an express ticket, but the Portuguese word *direto* is not the Brazilian equivalent of *express.* We made various stops. One was Coruripe, where my Peace Corps colleague Derek lived and worked. He wouldn't recognize it today. Coruripe has grown multifold since 1970, when I visited Derek and joined him for horseback riding through the coastal brush. The town now had a new, beautifully landscaped bus station.

Then it was on to Piaçabuçu, a dirty Alagoan hamlet in my time. That town, like Coruripe much improved, was throbbing with nocturnal life, the long *praças* crowded with people in a weekend festive spirit.

Street vendors were set up as if for midmorning. Radios blared, competing with live musicians. Through the open windows of the *Prefeitura* (Town Hall) I saw a meeting going on, its oratory stentorian. Every *praça* in town was alight and alive. Nobody moping at home alone in Piaçabuçu. There was life, community, and romance in the *praças* tonight.

As we approached Penedo, I wondered whether we might drive past my *sítio*. I spotted several places that looked like it. But, no, I lived in the highlands of Penedo. The bus had not climbed much; we were coming in from the coast.

At last, about three hours after departure from Maceió, we entered Penedo.

I stared through the dark with concentrated excitement.

At the first few stops the driver made to let passengers off, the town seemed unfamiliar. But, when we got into the *cidade histórica*—the old town, the nucleus—, it was very familiar, indeed. The central *praças*, the *Prefeitura*, the urban villas of the well-to-do, the radio station, the great monastery of São Francisco, the cathedral, the steep descent to the river...Yes, I knew that Penedo well.

Back in Penedo, after twenty-five years! My first arrival here was chance; this one is *destino*, an autobiographical inevitability. *Vou matar estas saudades*, ('I will quench this nostalgia').

I had assumed that the bus would stop on Avenida Floriano Peixoto, the main street and site of my Hotel São Francisco. Instead, the bus plunged down the hill, sailed through the riverside promenade, and landed in its terminal, down by the warehouses, about ten blocks and very much downhill of my hotel.

Mock me for my insistence that "I like to carry my stuff myself." As I sweated with my belongings, now augmented by further pounds of *lembranças*, including my *jangada*, a boatload, how I longed for a porter to help me up that hill. What a nice tip I would have had for him. What gratitude I would have felt for a helping hand!

Saturday, April 1. Penedo.

I don't know how it happened that I have arrived at every single stop of my trip in the dark of night. After mind-clearing sleep, I have then been able to see each place with fresh, auroral perceptions.

Saturday morning, Penedo at its peak! For today is the *feira* (market day), when all the residents of the town, its suburbs and rural abodes, and those who live on both riverbanks of the Rio São Francisco converge on Penedo for a day of frenzied buying and selling.

The vendors work a variety of venues. There are the huge, warehouse-like, market buildings, with long counters on which meat or produce is displayed to those who file through. There are also storefronts open to the street.

But the *feira* is not contained by buildings. The vendors sell from the back of open trucks, or from wooden carts or steel wheelbarrows. They operate out of sidewalk stands shaded by black plastic, or on rickety tables, or, lacking those, on a sheet of plastic laid on the granite-block pavement.

You would think that the sellers would set up their display and let the customers come to them. But, no, there are two strategies of selling. Some sellers are indeed stationary, but others mill in the streets, wandering about and shouting their offerings, obstructing the free passage of the customers. Boys carry trays of wares supported by a strap around their neck.

Wouldn't the itinerant peddlers see the same number of people, if they just stood still? Wouldn't that be a more effective presentation of their goods? I would think that the wandering Popsicle salesboy might become overheated and dip too much into his own stock, or, worse, get his stock all melted. Better if he found a shady spot, stood there, and shouted, *«Picolé!»*.

The fruits and vegetables of the *feira*, in all their colors, shapes, and sizes, in all their forms and varieties, are as tasty to the eye as to the tongue. The selection includes fruits generally not available in an American supermarket: *carimbola, pitanga, maracujá, jabuticaba, jaca, caju.* The tropical cornucopia is spilled into the streets of Penedo on *feira* day.

Less savory is the meat department. Here the head of a pig, its eyes shut tight in its last wince, there a row of bovine hearts—(not still beating, thank God!)—, a pile of livers, and a tableful of intestines. A large tongue lolls over the edge of the table. The stench of blood and offal rises in the crowded heat. It's enough to turn you into a vegetarian.

Nonetheless, if your stomach is as strong during the looking as in the eating, there are some choice cuts here. Brahma steaks in abundance, cut to your specifications.

I saw a butcher drop the fat and waste from his work into the basket of an old beggar woman.

Do you like chicken? Take your choice: A live one you can carry off flapping; one with its throat slit but still feathered; one cleaned and gutted; or any selection of poultry parts, even a clump of feet, if you fancy them. You can buy some live chicks to take home and raise for some future meal, perhaps when the in-laws drop in on a non-*feira* day. I heard the parting squawk of a cock just executed on a customer's orders. There was murder most fowl in Penedo this morning.

Due to the town's geographical location, the *feira* of Penedo can offer both seafood and riverfood. There are plenty of delectable piranhas or *tucunarés*; but some of the river fish had a crude, unappetizing look, like carp. There was fish fresh (the little *peixe-gatos* still panting on the dry ground) or dried-and-salted. Also, crabs, lobster, and shrimp. If you want to buy seafood in the *feira* of Penedo, I suggest you shop early, for it all sits in the sun, and such a slow cooking, I fear, does not enhance its flavor.

If, by philosophical conviction or mere squeamishness, you do incline toward vegetarianism, the *feira* will cater to your scrupulous diet. Besides the innumerable fruits and vegetables, there are grains and roots and tubers and beans and nuts and twigs and sprigs. Also, medicinal, even aphrodisiac, herbs, powders, and potions.

If, on the other hand, you scorn health consciousness and love self-indulgence, you can buy fresh tobacco cut in sections from a coiled rope. The vendor will even set it afire for you to experience and approve its aroma.

The *feira* is not a supermarket only. It provides every essential or frivolity you need or want or can be talked into needing and wanting. Down the street we go, past cosmetics and toiletries, housewares and hardware, watches and electronics, toys and *miudezas* (notions) of every kind. Around the corner to clothes and shoes. Then farther on to furniture, antiquey junk, machinery, and this-and-that.

How about a birdcage, with or without bird? I talked to a birdseller a few minutes. He told me the names of the kinds of birds he sells, imitated their repertoire, and said that listening to the radio was a great stimulus and inspiration to their singing. 'And does that one over there know any of the songs of Roberto Carlos?', I asked him, alluding to Brazil's most famous pop singer. No, the bird hadn't yet advanced to that level of cultural sophistication.

The vendors' product line may include a hundred items or only one, like the razor blades sold by one itinerant vendor. He offered me some, but I tugged at my beard and told him, *«Não preciso»*, ('Don't need 'em'). He laughed and moved on to more likely prospects.

The *feira* of Penedo has it all...well, except for diamonds and furs. You'll have to make do with junk jewelry; and the climate makes furs ridiculous, anyway.

The *feira* sprawled through the streets of an entire neighborhood; it was many times the area it used to be in my time of residence here. Last night, the desk clerk told me that Penedo has about 90,000 people, a threefold increase since I left, I think. The *feira* has grown accordingly. For those in search of sensory stimulation, the *feira* is the must-see-and-do attraction of Penedo.

As I walked the streets of the *feira*, I tried not to be the conspicuous outsider, I tried to mingle with the crowds. It is not easy for me to pass myself off as a *penedense*, for I tower over almost everybody. My three weeks of Brazil tan did provide some disguise, as did my dark sunglasses obscuring my bright blue eyes. Still, I drew some stares from the vendors and shoppers.

Perhaps I deserved their suspicious scrutiny. The sellers and the buyers of the *feira* must have thought me a strange stranger, for I spent the entire morning there—in two forays, with a breather between—, the entire Saturday morning, and yet I bought...nothing!

* * * * *

On my way to the *feira*, I would pass near the Hotel Magestic (pronounced in Brazilian Portuguese, *ma-jess-tee-kee).*

I believed I remembered which street to turn on to get there. In any case, the Magestic must be quite close, just two or three blocks away from my hotel. I recall that you could look out the window of the Magestic down onto the first stalls of the course of the *feira*.

When I came to Penedo in 1968, the first building I entered was the Hotel Magestic. Despite its grandiloquent name, it was just a boardinghouse, but a most homey one. And when Maria Heléna, the daughter of the owner, fell in love with me, the Magestic became my house of refuge from the stresses and adversities of Peace Corps life. In Maria Heléna's arms, I was no alien. I belonged.

I found the building, but not the Magestic. The corner part of it had been faced with new brick and was now occupied by a boutique.

I stood across the street in the shade and surveyed the building from one end to the other. No matter the changes wrought by time, this was a sacred place in my nostalgia pilgrimage.

My first month in Penedo, I lived in the Magestic, before I set up independent housekeeping on my *sítio*. Now, fixing upon the weathered shutters of the room I had occupied, I had an image, or almost an hallucination: The shutters swung open, and, from inside the Magestic, I of half my lifetime ago looked out.

I drew back into a doorway. I didn't want to be seen

by myself, for each one of myself should be ashamed of the other. I felt a fleeting fright at the encounter, face-to-face, of myself and my past.

I walked down the sidestreet a bit farther. The bicycle shop that was owned by Maria Heléna's father was still there, but it had a new owner, who told me that Maria Heléna's father had died. His second wife, whom I didn't know, still lived nearby.

The other end of the hotel was abandoned and crumbling, the doors of the rooms opened into nothingness. The sunken garden had been filled in with streetfront shops under a slapdash corrugated roof.

I made bold to walk into the boutique, where I met the owner of the building. She had inherited it from her father, who had neglected it, she said. The boutique was her attempt at rehabilitation.

I explained to her my connection with the Magestic and its previous family. She knew of the family, but could give me no specific information, except that she thought they were now all in Recife.

She gave me permission to visit, so I made my way down the dark corridor.

The back of the building looked like an earthquake had hit, although Brazil suffers no earthquakes. There were heaps of rubble on the tiled floor. Old, rotten doors, rusty grillwork, broken roof tiles, timbers, and pieces of fractured plumbing were lying all about.

I stood where the dining room had been, and I heard the voices of those congenial family evenings. I walked out to the veranda, where the caged dove used to coo and prance when Maria Heléna talked to him. And he would submit to her touch only.

The veranda had slender Ionic columns supporting the roof; they still stood but were badly weathered. Balusters from the railing were lying in a pile in the corner, like logs arranged for a funeral pyre.

I then entered where I had never been before, the dark private bedroom of a marriage of estrangement. The faded wallpaper still adhered to the wall. Above me, from its upside-down perch, a bat chirped in alarm at my intrusion into its abode.

I stood alone, amidst rubble. All around me, deterioration, decay, collapse, disintegration. And death.

The Hotel Magestic was a ruin. My past was a ruin.

* * * * *

In the pool of the Hotel São Francisco, I cooled my overheated body, but not by much, for, as the sun had beat upon the water all day, the pool was closer to tepid soup than to just melted glacier.

Later, the sun having withdrawn to the western horizon, I ventured out. *Passeando* (just strolling around) is the typical pastime of a small town like Penedo. I remember that the locals even used to take their caged birds for a walk.

I descended to the riverside promenade. Now below the horizon across the river, the sun pinked up the clouds in the west.

I found the Rio São Francisco very low at this time, the end of the dry season. In the flats below the rock embankment, young men played games of volleyball and soccer. The river had indeed been down for a long time, for, as the soccer players kicked at the ball, they kicked up puffs of dust.

Then there happened one of those happy little encounters with the locals. As I walked down the promenade, I walked past a young couple who had walked past me before. The young man greeted me with the time of day, and I returned the friendliness. He asked me where I was from, I told him, and he said that he had guessed me out, for he had had a lot of experience guiding foreigners. I told him that I was not wholly a foreigner.

The three of us then did our *passeio* together. Rogério was originally from São Paolo, but had moved to Penedo, where he worked in, of all fortunate coincidences, the Municipal Office of Culture and Tourism. He had studied English for eleven years, he told me, more than half his life, as I estimated. We exchanged a brief conversation in English, but I, the Berlitz teacher, evaluated his competence as poor. Nonetheless, Rogério himself taught English here in Penedo. Well, this is a provincial town. Not many fluent cosmopolites in Penedo.

His *namorada* was Adélebra, who got her name, she claimed, from a deceased sister of Barbra Streisand. Adélebra was born here in Penedo, but her father had moved the family around a lot. Because of her frequently changed residences, Adélebra was behind in her schooling; she seemed ashamed about it. Not a word of English did Adélebra know, so she was relieved when Rogério and I dropped our alien babel and reverted to Portuguese.

I explained to him that I had lived here long ago and wanted to get reacquainted with Penedo. Since they were just *passeando* and so was I, Rogério offered to show-and-tell me a few nearby sites.

The three of us ascended to the Praça Barão de Penedo, the historical plateau where, in 1637, invaders, determined that the *penedenses* would speak not Portuguese but Dutch, had built a fort to try to secure Penedo for *Brasil Holandês*. Penedo was the periphery of the Portuguese-Dutch struggle for Brazil that we saw back in Olinda.

The fort is gone, demolished by the pacific *penedenses*. In the *praça* today there is the *Prefeitura*, an eighteenth-century building called the *Aposentadoria*, which once included the public jail but now houses senior citizens, opposite that a small oratory where the condemned prayed all night before being led out of town for their hanging, and, completing the rectangle of the *praça*, the great cathedral, Nossa Senhora do Rosário dos Pretos.

We went into the cathedral, which was all illuminated outside and within, in anticipation of the Saturday evening Mass. Rogério and Adélebra conducted me through the church and its main chapel, the Santíssimo Sacramento.

The two of them alternated their descriptions and explanations, in a compatible antiphon. How different from the pestilential so-called guides infesting the streets of Olinda. Rogério and Adélebra were not scheming to pick my pockets. They were sharing their knowledge of their beloved town.

They then took me to the *Aposentadoria* and gave me a guided tour. Not much there, really...a few pieces of furniture, some ceramics, and an inscription in old Portuguese. The second floor featured a belvedere for a lovely dark panorama of the Rio São Francisco valley upriver.

They offered to accompany me to further sites of interest, but, as I saw Rogério give Adélebra a loving hug from behind, I told them that I was tired from all my itineraries of the day.

I did promise to look up Rogério in his office next to the *Prefeitura* and accept his future guidance.

Then I left them, to their Saturday night together, with each other.

Sunday, April 2. Penedo.

As I walked through the *feira* yesterday, I heard a young man using a microphone to make his pitch over the hurly-burly of the crowds. I was curious to see what he was selling, so I turned my course toward him.

As I got closer, I saw him and his microphone and a huge loudspeaker, but no tableful of wares. I heard the word *Salvador* several times. Was he doing tourist promotion for the capital of the state of Bahia?...Or was he a hypnotist, entertainer, or purveyor of quack cures? What was he selling, he that seemingly had nothing to sell?

Then I heard the first full sentence I understood, in Portuguese of course, but it might as well have been in English: 'Who wants to step up, right now, and receive Jesus Christ as your Lord and Savior (*Salvador)*?'

So, it was religion in the marketplace, like Paul in the *agora* of Athens.

As I listened to his spiel, I could have taken every sentence, put it into English, then into the mouth of a religious huckster on TV-38 in Chicago. Word-for-word, idea-for-idea.

In my hotel room, there is one of the 500 million Gideon Bibles, Portuguese edition. You know what it says, even if you're weak in languages. 'The way to salvation...Peace in time of trouble...Courage in time of fear...Strength in time of temptation...', and so on, followed by the appropriate references to particular scripture verses, which you could probably quote even before you look them up.

I don't know why Gideons think that people check into a hotel to seek salvation. Yet, there is that idle time in a hotel, and homesickness, and loneliness. Solitaries in a hotel become, I suppose, desperate for solace. Hotels may have saved more souls than churches have.

Anyway, regarding the *feira evangelion* and the Gideon Bible text, you might argue that they are exact translations, meant to be so; why shouldn't they be easily translatable back?

Yes, as a historian, I marvel at how translatable Judeo-Christianity has been through time and over multicultural distance. We long thought Communism its only serious modern rival, but we now see Communism struck mute. Islam will not move Westward; it is too culture-bound, and, of course, our women won't stand for it. No, the pitchmen from Palestine have been the only successful polyglots. If new contemporary ideological rival we would look for, I might nominate the thought system and methodology of American marketing, advertising, and promotion, the cultic consumerism now so pervasive everywhere.

I am no linguist, but I know some French, Italian, this current Portuguese, my own English, and a little German. What strikes me when I read or hear some idea in a particular language is how that same idea might just as well have come from any one of the other languages I know.

In my youth, when I studied linguistics, I was convinced of the Sapir-Whorff hypothesis of psycholinguistic determinism, which states that the structure of a language determines the contents of thought possible in that language. Now, however, I wonder whether worldwide intercommunication has overcome that determinism. Every idea I hear seems like a verse of the Gideon Bible, translatable, indeed already translated.

Of course, each language has its own structure, idiom, grammatical limitations, and vocabulary rich or poor. Despite all that, I have come to believe that everybody everywhere is saying the same thing. The *feira* evangelist in Penedo may serve as the type of the contemporary communicator, electronic amplification and all. His language is not Brazilian Portuguese; it is worldspeak.

How rare—and delightful—to encounter a statement so peculiar that it could only have come from the peculiarities of the language in which it was conceived. Alas, most of what I hear is not French *bon mot*, Latin terse epigram, Italian cynicism, Chinese gnome, or other linguistic uniqueness, but, rather, the hackneyed worldspeak.

When I first came to Brazil, some locals tried to entertain me with *piadas portuguesas*, Portuguese jokes; but they were the exact same Polish jokes I heard as a boy, including the one about three changing the lightbulb—one holding the bulb, the other two turning the ladder. One naive *penedense* even asked me whether we had Coca-Cola in the United States. He is not the only one to be a believer in local uniqueness, ignorant of ubiquity.

I read a Brazilian newspaper, and it might as well be a Chicago one. Brazilian TV news programs, too, are familiar in format and content: After the reporter does a piece, the anchor interviews the reporter (now become an expert on the subject), and the two have their little discussion, of which the viewer is an eavesdropper. And what they say is the same old thing. Damn worldspeak.

Wait a minute. Haven't I long been an advocate of the ideal of cosmopolitanism? Yes, but I never thought it would be reduced to this—a cosmopolitanism of banality.

"I should like to do away with language altogether," said Goethe the writer. Well, that time has come. All has been said, the same thing over and over again, in all the languages, and there is nothing more to be said. Let's all shut up and enjoy the peace of a wordfree, thoughtfree, speechfree head. Ah, silence!

. . . Now, having exhorted all to shut up, I must obey my own directive. . . .

That's it, a writer's Sunday sermon.

* * * * *

I walked over to the *Rocheira*. The *Rocheira* is an outcrop of rock that stands high over the Rio São Francisco. A natural citadel, it has been aptly compared, by our local historian Ernani Méro, to the Acropolis of Athens, because security is the enabler of culture. The community of Penedo–(the name means Big Rock)– had its origins on the *Rocheira*.

I entered a little alley to find where my Peace Corps colleague Mark used to live in a two-room rowhouse. I discovered the rowhouses now gone, replaced by the single block of a huge restaurant.

I continued to the cliff. I remember the garbage that covered the declivity, for the residents of the alley just toss their trash over the edge. The hillside used to be crawling with rats. I didn't look down long enough to determine whether that was still so. Anyway, the rats don't like the hot sun any better than the other residents of the *Rocheira*. They usually move about at both ends of the day. Rats or not, the beautiful flowering trees rising from the base of the cliff were festooned and draped with trash.

I turned left and followed a short alley not dissimilar to the one Mark had lived on. It descended slightly to another overlook of the river. The alley had the usual stench of urine. A sleepy little girl in a doorway roused herself to stare at me as I passed.

Looking down to the river's edge, I saw some women washing, or at least wetting, clothes from some flat rocks sloping down to the water. A man flung some kind of bait, tethered to a line, out into the stream.

I spotted, in the full of the flow, two heads bobbing, teen boys taking a swim. They were far from shore, and the current carried them along swiftly. They called to people on the shore and shouted that they were going to swim all the way to Neópolis, the next town downriver. One boy faked drowning, flailing his arms and submerging himself. I thought it a dangerous Sunday sport they were engaging in, for, as far out as they were and so swift the current, if one of them got into trouble, a boat could scarcely be launched in rescue before the boy would have gone down the requisite three times, perhaps clutching at, and pulling down with him, his hapless chum.

The family at the edge of the alley had a little walled pen for their pigs, right on the edge of the river. I wonder whether the pigs had any appreciation for their accommodations, there on the porcine riviera.

Retracing my steps, I went into one more alley coming from the cliff. It ran parallel to the alley where Mark had lived...or, rather, was this the alley he lived on?

If so, his house was still there, one of the ones in the row. There, that little blue one, #34, looked like his. Wasn't that the same pale blue paint, now scuffed and stained with a quarter-century of further habitation? The houses so similar, the two alleys so close, memory imprecise...I wasn't sure.

At the upper end of the alley, whom should I see leaning out a window in Sunday sociability but our chambermaid of the Hotel São Francisco. We exchanged recognition and greetings. Was today, her day off, to be spent in cleaning her own house? Well, it looked like a much lesser task than her job, judging by the size of her house.

—(I deduced from the maid's wet, bedraggled head yesterday, when I met her in the hallway coming out of the vacant adjacent room, that she avails herself of the hotel's facilities for her personal hygiene. Why not? A luxurious shampoo and a lolling bath in fine surroundings, a fringe benefit of her otherwise low-paying and menial job. I've yet to encounter her in the pool, however.)—

Then it was downhill to the church of Nossa Senhora da Corrente, Penedo's greatest cultural treasure, called by no less a personage than the director of the Louvre the most beautiful church in all Brazil.

Built in 1764, merely as a private chapel for a family named Lemos, the Corrente is an eye-popper of architectural and decorative extravagance. It mixes up, my young guide told me, Baroque, Rococo, and Neo-Classicism. Whatever the academic classificatory terminology, the altar is something you wouldn't expect to find in the Western world; it looks more like homage to Vishnu than to Jesus of Nazareth.

In my time, the Corrente had been abandoned and locked. One day, Mark and I did succeed in ferreting out the man who had the key, so that we could look into the church. Opening the rarely opened door and letting in unaccustomed sunlight, we flushed hundreds of bats to panicked flight. The atmosphere of the inside was pungent with their excretions. Those conditions made our visit voluntarily brief.

Now, however, the church of the Corrente is opened every day for inspection by locals and tourists. No religious services are held there; the Corrente is in the custody of the secular administration of the municipality of Penedo.

My guide, a black girl named Gilmara, showed me a secret door in the wall, where, she said, the Lemos family, staunch abolitionists, would hide and give refuge to runaway slaves. Brazil was slaveholding until 1888.

There was a Lemos grave under a marble slab in front of a side altar and open boxes of Lemos bones in a side room. Gilmara picked up a brown skull and turned it over, as if examining a melon at the *feira.*

She and I tried to make out the funerary inscriptions on the boxes; they were in archaic Portuguese, but, as we were familiar with funerary formulas and had only the puzzle of old spellings, we had little difficulty in our decipherment.

Of all those boxes of bones, one disassemblage must have been the last of the Lemoses, for, Gilmara informed me, the family is extinct. It's hard to imagine a Brazilian family line becoming extinct, but the Lemoses were apparently fervent in their religiosity, which may explain their attenuated fecundity.

As Gilmara turned away to greet another visitor, I made acquaintance with a woman named Francisca, who was, she told me, the director of a little museum called the Casa do Penedo. We discussed Penedo, its past, present, and prospects.

Francisca had little confidence in the future of tourism in Penedo. Too much filth and decay everywhere, she complained. And there are not 90,000 *penedenses*, as the municipal tourist brochure claims; more like 60,000. The *Prefeitura*, according to Francisca, was good-for-nothing. The last mayor she described as *analfabeto* (illiterate), but whether she meant that as insult or simple statement of fact I wasn't sure.

Francisca was escorting an old lady around town. The old lady was from Maceió, yet this was the first time in her long life that she had set foot in Penedo and seen its renowned Corrente church. There, that was exactly the problem. If Penedo couldn't attract tourists from Maceió, how could it draw them from Rio, São Paulo, or the United States?

What was there to do in Penedo, really? You look at a handful of churches; then what? Even the traditional festivals, that local color tourists seek, have become tawdry. *Feio* (ugly) was the word Francisca used.

Francisca has been in Penedo twelve years and has seen few changes for the better, she said. I myself could double her chronology and still might agree with her judgment.

We bid farewell, and I ascended the hill in search of more churches, which should be active this Sunday morning. In Nossa Senhora do Rosário dos Pretos, I found a service-of-sorts being conducted by a group of women. They all wore a red sash, members of some sodality perhaps. There was no priest in sight, there, in the cathedral itself, on a Sunday morning.

The tall green doors of the great church of the São Francisco monastery were shut.

Then, a shock and further disappointment, I came across the little Cine Penedo, like the Magestic an abandoned ruin now discovered on my local itineraries. Mark and I had attended many a film showing there. Mark was prophetic in his anticipation that movies, television, and other visual media would become dominant in our culture, and that books would count for little.

On the Rua Sete de Setembro, I looked for the printshop once owned by *seu* Manoel, the landlord of my *sítio*. I used to drop in there for my mail and to pay my rent and to visit with his grandson, who was raising a huge flock of pigeons. But I could find neither print-shop nor even the address I remembered.

Descending the hill, I happened to pass Gilmara coming up. 'On your way to lunch?', I asked her. Yes, she was. So was I.

* * * * *

While having lunch in the restaurant of the Pousada Colonial, I was treated to a sample of Brazilian television. It was a stunt show, with an effusive, money-dispensing host, attended by shapely models and playing to a screaming, clapping audience. There were dancing mascot characters and nonstop happy music.

In the first stunt, a helicopter flew over Copacabana Beach and parachuted down a package that burst open, scattering money. The entertainment consisted in watching the bathers scramble through the surf after the cash.

Next, it was a maze that dogs had to run, in order to earn money for their masters, who called or whistled to them from the exit and finish line. Few dogs could accomplish the task, for their doggy minds couldn't grasp the idea of getting where one wanted to go by running off in some other direction. Some dogs tried to vault the wall, but it was too high, even for the Great Dane. There were mirrors in the barriers, meant to confuse further.

One little pooch expressed his frustration by lifting his leg and leaving his opinion of it all on a corner of the maze. The next competitor started off running and searching, but then got distracted by the scent on the wet wall. A few dogs did find their way out of the maze, more by persistent random running than by any canine cogitation.

In the third stunt, we were presented with two athletic young men and two voluptuous young women, all in bathing suits. But they were covered in mud, alas. So, a female contestant, equipped with a turned-on garden hose and a sponge, endeavored to clean the men, while a male contestant tried likewise to clean the women. What with the sponging of every muscle and curve and the directed flow of the hose's water toward every muddy orifice, it was, in all, a fine piece of pandering, whichever gender you preferred to direct your personal lust toward. I was waiting for a male contestant to stick the hose into a swimsuit and, with such explicitness, come clean on what it was all supposed to mean.

In the last stunt, a chimpanzee stood on a high wall

and flung down at the contestants dinner plates one after another. The contestant earned so much per plate he or she was able to catch, nothing for those that fell short or sailed over to crash on the pavement beyond. The chimpanzee was cooperative in his willingness to fling the plates, but he had an erratic arm.

And on it went, all that fun and money. A Sunday afternoon of time-killing diversion for the Brazilians.

The only one who managed to keep his dignity through the proceedings was the chimpanzee. Nobody could make a monkey out of him, because he already was one.

*****

The casanova of the sidewalk bar, seated at his accustomed table, managed to stop a casual acquaintance of his as she was passing by.

She leaned against a post and looked down upon him and his intentions.

'That's a cute little nose you've got,' he said to her.

She answered, matter-of-factly, 'It was broken.'

Monday, April 3. Penedo.

'*Senhor* Peixoto was a visionary,' *dona* Francisca said to me. 'When he built the Hotel São Francisco, not even Recife had a hotel like that.'

Financed by the profits of the textile mill he owned across the river, with funds added by *senhor* Gonçalves and other partners, on land donated by the municipality, the new Hotel São Francisco rose up from the dirt of Penedo.

The governor of Alagoas had tried to convince *senhor* Peixoto to build the hotel in Maceió, but *senhor* Peixoto was a local patriot. He would build his grand hotel in Penedo and, by doing so, propel Penedo into a future prosperity of tourism and economic development.

The project began in 1956, and construction continued until 1962. Built on a height, the six-story hotel would command, from the balconies fronting its rooms, panoramic vistas of the old town and the Rio São Francisco. The hotel itself was an imposing, beautiful, pink work of art.

Inside, there was an elegance in the style of the time. Shiny surfaces, sweeping curves of walls, a spiral staircase (mostly for looks; the hotel had the only elevator in Penedo), bright artwork, walls of paneled wood squares, parquet floors, air conditioning. Everything the most modern and best available.

Services to guests included restaurant and bar, barber and beauty shops, ice-cream parlor, boutique, in-house laundry, newsstand, and a splendid cinema that seated a thousand. Later, a swimming pool would be added.

The hotel would host regional development conferences, conventions, live entertainment presentations—(even Roberto Carlos performed in the cinema)—, and an international film festival.

Yes, the Hotel São Francisco had it all. Except customers.

I remember that, when I first arrived in Penedo—(the hotel only six years old at the time)—, I asked myself the obvious question, Why is there a hotel like that in a place like this? *Senhor* Peixoto's zealous local boosterism lacked common sense.

This week, only eighteen of the fifty-two rooms of the hotel are occupied. That's the problem. That has always been the problem.

With such a slim stream of revenue from guests, it is not surprising that the hotel is sinking into dilapidation. In my room, the air conditioner works, but it has been jerry-rigged with patched wiring (which is alarmingly warm) and a transformer on the floor. The connection of the hose that was supposed to drain off the condensed water has crumbled away; the water was just dripping onto the balcony, until I got a plastic pail from the maid. The lock on the door doesn't work from the inside, and the knob is hard to turn. The glass doors to the balcony slide open only after a tug-of-war. Pieces of the parquet floor are detached for me to trip over, and the wood veneer in the armoires is turning into paper. It looks like the bidet was used as a dump by painters, the toilet valve sticks...and so on.

When, back in the States, I read in the guidebook that Penedo hosted an international film festival, I hoped it wouldn't be going on while I was here, for, if so, how could I get a room? But no need to worry. The

Cinema São Francisco is shut down. Its air conditioning was busted, the projection machine was always on the fritz, there weren't that many customers anyway, the desk clerk told me. No, don't worry about the crowds at the Penedo International Film Festival, because there isn't a single operating cinema left in Penedo.

Besides the cinema, other services of the hotel have fallen into disuse; there is no barber or beauty shop. A uniformed doorman stands sentinel, but stands is about all he has to do. The restaurant, however, is still open; I enjoyed an excellent shrimp-in-coconut-sauce there yesterday.

There are some positive aspects to the state-of-things in the Hotel São Francisco. When I made my reservation, how I wanted a room at the top overlooking the river! In a mostly empty hotel, that was a request not hard to grant. I'm on the top floor, facing the river, just as I had hoped. The best room in the hotel, the best hotel room in all Penedo. Moreover, the place is quiet; and I usually have the little swimming pool all to myself.

The Hotel São Francisco stands as a symbol of Penedo and its civic boosters. Beauty amidst squalor, elegance where there is little culture, modernity forced upon the rustic, investment in the quixotic, optimism over nothing.

* * * * *

I stopped into a stationery store on Avenida Floriano Peixoto to buy a notebook, having nearly exhausted the pages of mine with my voluminous effusions.

I got into a little chat with the clerk and another young woman standing by. There was a huge map of North America on the wall; Penedo, like the rest of the world, looks toward the United States. I showed them where I was from, and I told them that my name, Norman, means *man from the north*, which, in my case, described me perfectly.

The young woman, it turned out, was born and grew up right near my old *sítio*. She was twenty-nine years old, she said, so she must have been one of those half-naked, cute and dirty, little urchins I used to pass when walking or bicycling to and from my house. She described the neighborhood by reference to its principal landmark, a *chafariz*, which I remembered well. That source of water was a site of neighborly mingling.

She rattled off the names of the neighbors of that time, many still there, she said. Did I remember a *dona* Rosa? 'Was she fat?,' I asked. Yes, she is fat. Well, then, perhaps I did remember her. The woman said she would mention my name around to see whether any of the neighbors remembered me.

I bid the two young ladies a good-day and descended the hill to return to the church of the Corrente to photograph its decorative extravagances.

Gilmara smiled and greeted me from the steps. She is a good-looking negress, or *mulatta*. (In Brazil, despite the dozens of Portuguese terms the Brazilians use to categorize themselves by race, any description of type is necessarily imprecise.) Gilmara's black skin is shiny, like enamel.

She has an amiable temperament. As she accompanied me around again, my jokes and jests made her laugh a lot. Why should history and art always be burdened with heavy-handed seriousness?

I asked Gilmara whether I might ascend one of the two bell towers. She herself had not been up there, she said; she had only worked as a guide in the Corrente for a month. Maybe the steps were rotten, and, anyway, she was afraid of heights.

I cajoled her and reassured her, until the two of us began the ascent.

Several flights of wooden steps, acceptable in their solidity, led up the tower, the one with the bells. (It was the right tower, not the left one, as shown in the reverse-printed photo in the town's tourist brochure. I joked with Gilmara about 'The Miracle of the Corrente,' when angels came by night to transfer the bells from one tower to the other, because that was the way God preferred them.)

The bells were bronze, three in number, one of them, I read on the engraving, made in Lisbon in 1802.

I pulled on the clapper of the first bell. It sounded a clear tone reverberated from its slender form. The second bell was bigger and broader. When I pulled the clapper against its side, a tone deeper than that of the first sounded. Ready to hear the performance of the entire trio, I reached under the third bell, but found nothing there. Its tongue had been cut out. Singing no more, it now has to be a mute listener to the tonal proclamations of its two fellows.

Gilmara descended quickly. She loved the view from the tower, she said, but she was still a bit queasy about the altitude. I advised her to descend the steps facing upward, rather than down, as if on a ladder. Such a descent reduces vertigo, as every kitten should learn.

I shot my photos and further explored the church. On the way out, Gilmara showed me where the termites had eaten the roof beams. The municipality had tried to poison the termites out, but got around to it too late.

Clay roof tiles are very heavy. I hoped that the apocalyptic prophecy Jesus of Nazareth had directed toward the Temple of Jerusalem would not come to pass, belatedly, on the Penedo church of the Corrente. At least not, God forbid!, while my amiable guide is on duty within.

* * * * *

Next to the church of the Corrente, facing the riverside promenade, is a *sobrado* (multistory home) that once belonged to the wealthy Lemos family, then served as a junior high school. It has been beautifully restored and now operates as the Pousada Colonial.

If you want a charming and romantic abode in Penedo, the Pousada Colonial is the place to stay. Its only negative is that, with all the cars, buses, and trucks passing in front on their way to take the vehicle ferry across the river, and with the nightly gatherings in the *praça*, it might be a bit noisy.

I had enjoyed an excellent meal at the Colonial, so I walked over for another one. (I hoped the TV would not be on this time.)

The lobby of the Colonial is decorated with old photos and drawings of the landmarks of Penedo. On a table I happened to see a model of a ship, a double-decked old steamer. *Comendador Peixoto* was the name printed on its hull.

Could this be *the boat*, the one I remembered so well? About thirty years ago, it had been brought down from the Mississippi River, out into the Gulf of Mexico, Caribbean, Atlantic, and finally up the Rio São Francisco, where it stood floating along the riverside promenade of Penedo.

Why had it been brought here? The town was abuzz with ideas and speculations about its use. To conduct tourists on pleasure excursions up and down the river? A floating bar? A floating hotel? A floating office? To which my partner Mark added, as a Peace Corps volunteer, a floating school?, and, as a rascal, a floating brothel?

One day, Mark and I fenagled our way aboard. We examined its decks and cabins. It was old but solid steel from stem to stern. Yes, it had all kinds of utilitarian possibilities. Had I not been so contented with my life as a country squire on my *sítio*, I might even have liked to live on that old boat.

Mark and I would walk by the ship every day on our evening *passeio*. And every day it just stood there. Nobody aboard, no work being done on it, just idling, month after month.

Then, one evening, we were startled to see the ship three-quarters under water. The flowing river had rotted her steel hull, the stream had entered, and, in the dark of night, the ship had sunk into the mud.

Was this model in the Pousada Colonial, this *Comendador Peixoto*, that very ship? I called over the waiter and interviewed him about it. Yes, that was the very ship, he told me. Hadn't it been brought down from the Mississippi?, I asked, seeking confirmation of what I had been told. 'From the Missouri River,' the waiter said. Well, Mississippi and Missouri are two-into-one, like Rio Negro and Rio Solimões, so my story was essentially confirmed.

But wait a minute. The craftsman's name was on

the model, as was the date, 1994. How could the modelmaker reproduce the dimensions and appearance of a ship sunk twenty-five years before and probably salvaged or rotted since? Oh, he had worked from old photos, the waiter told me.

Returning to the dining room, the waiter introduced me to the diners as the American who had witnessed the sinking of the *Comendador Peixoto.*

Two men were at a table, leaning back against the wall, drinking their beer. They started asking me questions about the ship, and, in a moment, I had joined them at their table.

The first gentleman, *seu* Murilo, had an intelligent, foxy look, his alertness only slightly diminished by the alcohol in the beer he was drinking.

What was his profession?, I asked him, starting with a common topic of social inquiry.

Murilo made a gesture of helplessness, as if the question were impossible to answer. A long explanation would be necessary. He had started out as a priest, then turned truck driver. He had been a jurist, a farmer, a businessman, a wheeler-dealer, and a street vendor. Why, he had once donned bikini shorts to sell oranges on Copacabana Beach in Rio.

'You mean,' I asked him, 'that you were a priest in a bikini selling oranges on Copacabana Beach?' The other man laid his head back against the wall and enjoyed a hearty laugh at that imagery of his spindly friend.

What he really was, said Murilo, was an adventurer. He had been all over Brazil. He was mad about travel. Why, if he didn't have to pay his daughter's way through college, he wouldn't be here in Penedo working away. (At what? He never told me his current job). No, he'd be off sailing around the world.

Murilo looked at his watch with a startled expression and told his friend that he'd better be off. He made a gesture of his wife pulling on his ear, as if dragging a naughty boy home.

His friend Eric (a Nordic name, but pronounced in Portuguese as *EH-hickee*), prevailed upon him to stay. Eric was solid as a boulder, a *penedo* himself. He had a sunburned face that made him look like an Indian and the black beard of a highwayman. In fact, Eric was quite civilized, well-informed about the world, and articulate in his judgments and opinions.

Eric was a topographer, but we had no time to talk about what his work entailed, because he launched the three of us into a highly sophisticated discussion on a variety of economic and political topics.

We discussed the agricultural methods of Israel and the United States, compared to Brazil. Agricultural self-sufficiency and the economics of import and export. Development loans, deficits, and the prospects for a universal currency. American aid programs: USAID, the Alliance for Progress, and my own Peace Corps. American foreign policy since the Kennedy administration, especially toward Latin America (Fidel), and Vietnam. The military regime of Brazil, its retardation of national development.

Eric asked me to explain the American university system to him. Could he get into Harvard or Yale? I described the soaring costs of higher education and talked about scholarships.

Eric told me that the population figure of 90,000 for Penedo was pure fantasy. He himself had seen the most recent census figures. 52,000, that's all. As an interior Alagoas town of importance, Penedo fell behind Arapiraca long ago and was now being surpassed by Palmeira dos Índios.

I surprised myself by being able to hold my own in such a wide-ranging and sophisticated discussion. We three understood most of what we were hearing from one another.

I should have a talk and beer with his father, Eric suggested. His father had supervised the installation of Penedo's first telephone system.

Oh, and what about the *Comendador Peixoto*? Salvagers had stripped what they could for machinery and scrap steel, Eric told me, but a big piece of the hull was still there, where it sank twenty-five years ago. The river was low now. I could go down and see for myself.

I shook hands with my stimulating conversationalists and headed down to the river. Sure enough, a jagged piece of rusted steel protruded a few feet out of the water. I could discern an outline of more of it down in the mudbrown depths.

I saw some fish jumping and splashing around the wreck. They could rest from battling the current by taking refuge behind the reef of old steel. The *Comendador Peixoto* has found its use, at last.

* * * * *

Back in the hotel, I got a telephone call. I could barely hear the person calling. It was like two boys talking into cans at the ends of a taut string.

I think the system that Eric's father installed in Penedo is still in place. Or did he say it was his grandfather?

* * * * *

I may have had more social contacts these past three weeks in Brazil than I had this past year back at home in the States.

In a tropical country, people are always outside and, so, necessarily intermingling. And when you live in a rural area or small town, talk is the main pastime. A culture of sociability develops.

What does everybody talk about? One another, of course. Human interest—or gossip, as you may choose to call it—does have its negative aspect, as I myself once discovered to my chagrin. Do something terrible, and your shame will be broadcast. Counterbalancing that, your casual conversations will lead to useful information, valuable contacts, and human immersion into friendships and romance.

I confess that, in my Peace Corps days, I was impatient with small-town chit-chat. I would tire of it quickly, then retreat behind the palisade of my *sítio* to a learned book from my study. This second trip has demonstrated to me the error of my earlier ways. My daily conversations are more human and interesting than all the tomes of *Herr Doktor* Freud I used to read in solitary soliloquy.

On this trip I am promiscuous, but not in the way you'd expect, if you knew my reputation. My recent *Tropical Ecstasy* has been not sex, but socializing.

Tuesday, April 4. Penedo.

This early morning, the first heartening signs of the approach of the rainy season appeared, as heavy masses of lofty gray clouds advanced from the Atlantic inland.

The climatic scourge of the *sertão* (the interior of the *nordeste*) has been drought, sometimes for consecutive years. Penedo and the communities farther inland are now enduring the depths of the dry season. This time of year, the people of the *nordeste* look toward the Atlantic for its beneficence of rain.

They say that the rains must arrive by St. Joseph's Day, March 19, to ensure a fertile season. I encountered the tropical rains in Recife and Maceió, but here in the interior they are already more than two weeks late. Recent days have been hot and dry and mostly cloudless.

Today's auroral clouds produced only evanescent sprinkles, but perhaps they are harbingers.

On a stroll uphill, I saw the door to the great monastery of São Francisco open. I never pass an interesting open door without entering, because who knows if I will ever find it open again?

According to the state historian, Jayme de Altavila, this monastery was one of the three nucleuses of civilization in Alagoas.

I entered the Franciscan cloister, so reminiscent of those of Italy. Back further in time than medieval Christianity, to walk into a cloister is to enter a *peristylum* of a house on a fine pagan Roman villa.

Amid the trees and flowers and grapevines of the cloister was a cageful of doves, birds dear to St. Francis, here in forced confinement to a monastery, where, as I noticed, however, they did not practice celibacy.

The doves were the only residents of the monastery, as my young guide Adriano told me. A priest comes to say Mass in the church, Santa Maria dos Anjos, a caretaker cleans, and guides conduct visitors, but there are neither monks nor priests living within. This community of Franciscans, established here in 1660, is now extinct.

I have been to Assisi, to its monastery, to the sepulchre of St. Francis himself. *Francisco,* a name I hear over and over again in Penedo, applied to the river, to my hotel, to the local radio station, to this monastery, to some of the people I meet. An anachronistic name now, for it is not only the body of St. Francis that is buried, but the idea of monasticism itself. The monastery of São Francisco is a mausoleum of monasticism.

Adriano took me through the halls and rooms of the complex. Everywhere there was termite devastation and water damage, breakage and decay, neglect and abandonment.

A long section of carved and gilded ceiling molding, rotted from behind by moisture, had crashed to the floor of the church, just after a group of worshippers had left. I think there will be more collapse to follow.

The altar of Santa Maria dos Anjos is a Portuguese Baroque extravagance comparable to that in the Corrente. The simpler the lines, the simpler the maintenance. There are no simple lines in the Baroque, and I didn't see many signs of maintenance.

I sat on the steps of the altar and had a conversation with Adriano. He was born in Penedo, is nineteen years old, a student by night and guide by day, for which latter the municipality pays him the equivalent of thirty dollars a month.

Adriano asked me about studying English. And he wanted to talk about soccer and other sports in the U.S.

Finally, after a half-hour of conversation, Adriano apologized for bothering me with all his questions, especially because he is a guide, whose job it was to answer, not to ask, questions. I told him that I enjoyed satisfying his curiosity.

Shortly after I arrived back in my hotel, some steady rains arrived. For the first time in what I guess must have been many months, umbrellas appeared in the streets of Penedo.

* * * * *

One of the main topics of conversation during my two years in Penedo was the bridge.

The Rio São Francisco has been described as "the river of national unity". That would be apt, if the population of the country all lived riverside. In fact, the most populous cities of Brazil, state capitals, are on the seacoast. The Rio São Francisco obstructed transportation from south to north between the capitals. And there was no bridge across the São Francisco.

There was going to be one, financed in part, if I remember, by American aid money. But where would the bridge be built?

At Penedo was the most logical choice. Penedo was

the biggest town on the most direct route. It could provide needed services to travelers.

The bridge would funnel the flow of traffic, and therefore of business, into Penedo. Penedo's future depended on the bridge. Penedo had to have the bridge.

But the military regime of Brazil decided, for reasons that, I was told, were more military-strategic than economic-practical, to build the bridge far upstream, at Propriá, Sergipe. Penedo had lost out.

The bridge was only completed after my departure in 1970, so I never had the chance to gauge its effect on the economy of Penedo. When I asked *dona* Francisca her opinion, she said, 'Bridge, no bridge, I don't think it made any difference to Penedo.'

Now that there was a bridge at Propriá, I was surprised to find, upon my recent return, the huge ferries still transporting cars and buses and trucks across the river between Penedo and Sergipe. I asked Adriano about it.

He told me that the bridge at Propriá had begun to show cracks, so some people were afraid of it. Also, the road from the bridge was full of monstrous potholes, and, furthermore, you had to deviate far inland to use the bridge, adding to your travel time. Considering all that, some people still preferred to take the vehicle ferries at Penedo.

Dona Francisca's assessment of the bridge question was probably right.

One of the topics of this, my current, stay is the hydroelectric dams, Paolo Afonso and the new Xingó, upriver. The problem now is not the river as obstruction, but obstructions upon the river.

The volume of water at Penedo has been so reduced by the dams that the cultivation of paddy rice, which I remember as practiced in the lowlands of Penedo's Bairro Vermelho, is a fraction of what it used to be. On the flip-side, a few years ago the dam once released too much water too quickly, flooding the streets of Penedo, a dirty trick not of Nature upon humans, but of engineering Brazilians upon riverine townsfolk Brazilians.

Water is now the mere means to electricity, the flow of charged juice of higher priority than the flow of river commerce and culture.

In the future, will there be another bridge or another dam? To Penedo, the river will always matter.

* * * * *

Oh, Penedo, what are you? What is your future?

'I'm very proud to be *penedense,*' affirmed Gilmara. And when Adélebra's father brought up the possibility of moving the family once again, Adélebra, timid and submissive though she is, raised strenuous objections. She has been here in Penedo six years now. She wants to stay.

The people of Penedo have a civic loyalty and sentimental attachment to their community. A certain look of smittenness comes into their eyes when they merely mention the name, Penedo. *O nosso querido Penedo* ('our dear Penedo').

Yet, when they find out about my earlier residence here, they say «*"Piorou,"*» that is, everything is worse here now. And when I ask whether there is still commercial air service, or cinemas, or *jangadas* on the river, or a good bar on Avenida Floriano Peixoto, their response is the same, «*Acabou-se*» ('done for', 'gone'). They shake their heads at the current state of the town.

Many blame the municipal administration. My few days here would not incline me to contradict them.

To send a man out with handbroom, shovel, and wheelbarrow is no effective way to keep the streets clean, yet that is exactly what the *Prefeitura* does.

I spotted a brand-new van belonging to the *Prefeitura* bearing its officials, but the garbage truck could compete with the *Comendador Peixoto* in a rust contest. It was an open, flatbed truck with a crew of five. One drove, one ran alongside and flung the plastic bags of garbage, one stood atop the pile in high rubber boots, caught the bags and arranged them neatly at his feet, and two hung on the door next to the driver. The last two might spell the jogger at intervals. I can't say for certain that all five were municipal employees, of course, but it seems unlikely that two grown men would go joyriding on a garbage truck.

The other day, from the balcony of my room, I saw smoke at the side of São Gonçalo. Was the church burning? I heard no hubbub, so I withdrew. But that night, as I did a *passeio* of downtown, I happened into the narrow street along São Gonçalo. And there I passed by smouldering heaps of garbage, which had been set afire against the wall of São Gonçalo itself, one of the four ecclesiastical treasure-houses of Penedo. And the foul smoke wafted into a nearby restaurant. The locals treat their town as badly as does the municipal administration.

As I stood on the *Rocheira* last Sunday morning, a

young man passed and remarked to me, 'Beautiful view, isn't it?' Yes, but only if your eyes scan the distant horizon. If you let your gaze drop to the garbage strewn cliff, the aesthetic is spoiled. What good distant beauty, if you live amidst proximate ugliness?

I'm not a neat-freak, and, after all, I grew up in a neighborhood in Chicago. But when I went down to seek the wreck of the *Comendador Peixoto*, I sickened at the stench of the polluted mud and cast grieving eyes upon the litter tossed over the wall of the promenade. It's not just finicky nitpicking or eco-puritanism I'm expressing here. I'm talking about gross filth, vermin, and—(not so fantastic as you might think)—possible bubonic plague, or cholera, a half-dozen cases of the latter reported in Alagoas this month.

The *penedenses* love Penedo. I do, too. But how can any of us stand to look upon what Penedo has become? *Piorou. Acabou-se.*

'Tourism will be the salvation of Penedo!' I heard that refrain many times before, long ago. There are five banks in Penedo, but none, not even the great Banco do Brasil, has a *câmbio* in it. The Banco do Brasil had one in my time, but *acabou-se.* If only more tourists came to Penedo, a bank functionary told me, the Banco do Brasil would open a *câmbio.* I told him that he had it exactly backwards. When he offered the hope that the next time I came to Penedo I might find a *câmbio*, I told him bluntly, 'I doubt it.'

So, that's what you get in Penedo: Incompetent municipal administration, a contaminated environment, and a lack of essential services. I'd bet that the old lady from Maceió who was visiting the Corrente got out of town before nightfall.

What about the love of *penedenses* for their town? When I checked into the Hotel São Francisco, I noticed on the lobby wall a romantic oil painting of the Corrente in its setting. The artist's signature was M. Celina. Could this be the same Maria Celina, of the hotel family, whom I once taught English to as a Peace Corps volunteer? The very same, the desk clerk told me. I'd like to meet her and talk over old times, I said to him. That wasn't possible, he answered. Maria Celina had painted the proof of her sentimental love for Penedo and then moved away, to Recife.

In the luncheonette of the Hotel São Francisco, there is a wall clock. It says 5:20. The second-hand is at the 59-second mark. It twitches, twitches, twitches, but it never advances into the next minute. That is Penedo.

* * * * *

Whenever I tell the locals the story of my past connection with Penedo, the older ones, those who knew the time and can compare it to today, remark wistfully that Penedo was so much better then. I've been hearing the Portuguese equivalent of the refrain, "Those were the days...".

What, have I come here to Penedo, taking my nostalgia trip, only to provoke the *penedenses* to do the same?

Yet, it hardly seems right for someone on a nostalgia trip to criticize others for their mere sentimentality.

I need to balance the picture a bit. Further experience moderates the extremity of our judgments. This afternoon, I discovered a very constructive contribution to the community.

When I first met *dona* Francisca in the Corrente, she invited me to visit her Casa do Penedo. Some kind of pitiful little local museum, I assumed.

I found it while on one of my walking excursions. Its sign described it not as *museu*, but as *espaço cultural* (culture center). *Dona* Francisca was not in, but a colleague of hers welcomed me, answered my questions, and showed me around.

There was a *penedense*, a medical doctor, it seems, who left Penedo for Brasília. But he did not leave Penedo completely. He donated his house and considerable money to establish a center for the documentation of all aspects of the community of Penedo. The Casa do Penedo opened just two years ago.

As you go from room to room, you get, in old photos, documents, and artifacts, an overall view of Penedo through time. Subjects treated include important historical events, customs and mores at different periods, the changing townscape, the influence of the Rio São Francisco, Church history, the local educational institutions, native sons who made good one way or another, and so on.

Best of all, the Casa do Penedo has a research library on local history, complete with computer and printer. They even do document restoration. Open to everyone and welcoming everybody, the center is staffed by six people. The layout, the exhibits, the library, and the docent are all first-rate.

The geographical scope of the Casa do Penedo is, of course, narrow. Few outsiders would put it on their itinerary. Nonetheless, it is only by such an appreciative understanding of the past of their own town that *penedenses* can be stirred to civic action.

The Museu do Indio back in Manaus was about *them*; the Casa do Penedo is about *us*. The Casa do Penedo is not a repository of relics; it is a stream of living civic consciousness.

The docent told me that the Penedo public library was out-of-operation. Like so many others I have talked to, she criticized the municipal administration. What were its priorities?

That Penedo has no operating public library is a disgrace. That it now has the Casa do Penedo is a reason for justifiable local pride.

* * * * *

Her strong perfume, familiar to me, wafted through even before her arrival.

When she did walk by, the casanova of the sidewalk bar stopped her and complimented her on her legs, most all of which were on view below her short bluejean shorts.

He complimented her on her legs.

She showed him the back of them, receding.

Wednesday, April 5. Penedo.

Last night, at about 11:00 P.M., the electricity went out. Even a working air-conditioning unit depends upon a Higher Power. I woke up to find my room suddenly turned sultry and stuffy.

I staggered half-asleep out onto the balcony.

Below me, all Penedo was dark. Not only Penedo, but the river towns usually visible from the vantage point of my balcony. Slightly upriver on the other side, in Sergipe, Carrapicho, recently renamed Santana do São Francisco, had disappeared against its black hillside. Directly across from Penedo, Passagem, the opposite ferry landing, gone. Downriver, where I knew Neópolis stood, nothing was to be seen through the drizzle.

So, Paulo Afonso, the hydroelectric dam on the São Francisco, was not only taking away Penedo's water; it was failing to make recompense by delivering the juice.

In an upper window of the Pousada Colonial, a candle flickered. There, perhaps, power failure enkindled an opportunity for romance. Down in the *praça* by the river, someone had a light that shone bright red, as if a traffic light had sprung up in Penedo. And they must have lit a gas lantern in the lobby of the Hotel São Francisco, for the facade of the bank building opposite reflected a pale light. Except for those few individual initiatives, the streets of Penedo became as they must have been on some night a century ago.

The ferry was approaching. It had its own lights, but the captain had asked the trucker whose vehicle was in the bow to turn on his headlights, so that the captain could find the landing.

In a few minutes, the lights of Carrapicho went back on. To an arriving visitor from outer space, little Carrapicho would now have appeared as the only site of human life and civilization in the river valley.

Penedo had ceased to exist. In a street below me, a dog kept up a distressful barking and lament over what had happened.

I went back to bed. Sometime late in the night, the air conditioner came back to life, and, with the dawn, so did Penedo.

* * * * *

I saw a man in the park across the street from the hotel watering a flowering shrub with a hose. I was tempted to go down to him and tell him to stop an unnecessary labor and conserve the water, for a major rainfall was on its way from the Atlantic Ocean.

I, the stranger, was reading the signs of the environment, while the locals were oblivious to them. Actually, I had the advantage over the man with the hose, because, from the lofty eyrie of my hilltop sixth-floor room, I spotted the advancing clouds well before those down on the pavement among the buildings could. Anyway, he was engaged in conversation with a comrade; watering the shrub was just a way of including a third in the gathering.

There has been no rain to speak of for six months, Adélebra told me. Well, there will now be a substantial rain today.

The rains of the tropics are not the tentative, brooding, lingering ones we northerners are used to. No, tropical rains come in, drop a drench, then move on.

Between the downpours, the sky opens up, so there is usually sun on a rainy day, and, if wet, you will soon dry off.

The heaviest rainfall I ever saw in my life was in Arapiraca, here in Alagoas. The old cliché about not being able to see your hand in front of your eyes was virtually true. I felt submerged.

Penedo climbs up to heights from the riverbank. The town has no storm sewers to speak of, so, when it rains, great torrents stream down over the black paving blocks toward the river. The rains do a more efficient street cleaning than the municipal administration does.

Unfortunately, what cleans the town dirties the river. Penedo's litter, filth, and oily grime are carried down into the Rio São Francisco.

The landscape worker in the park might as well coil up his hose and put it away. Nature has relieved him of his job. The rainy season has come back to Alagoas, at last.

* * * * *

Murilo told me this joke:

God was working away at the Creation. He had just made Brazil.

The Archangel Michael looked down from the heavens upon Brazil. He flew over to where God was working.

"Excuse me, Your Highness," Michael said to God. "May I ask you a question?"

"Yes, yes," God said impatiently. (He didn't like to be interrupted in His work, especially on such an important project as the Creation.)

"I see you have made Brazil as a tropical paradise," said Michael. "You've given it sunshine in a warm climate, a beautiful landscape, all the fruits and foods of land and sea, beautiful beaches, great rivers. And you have spared it earthquakes and volcanoes and hurricanes and tornadoes and blizzards and such troubles that you gave other places you have made. Did you make Brazil perfect?"

"No," God answered. "Wait 'til you see the people I will put there."

* * * * *

I wanted to come to some further assessment of Penedo's economic situation, so I engaged the brother of the owner of the restaurant on the *Rocheira* in an after-dinner conversation on the subject. Francisco is aptly named for local pertinence. About my age and having lived in Penedo all his life, Francisco could provide me with both current information and historical perspective.

First, the base of the modern economy, industry and manufacturing. I knew that the textile and clothing factory across the river was still in operation, because the black smoke from its chimney began to drift up the river valley very early each morning.

My informant told me that only a minority of the workers there were *penedenses*. What with the low wages they were paid and the cost and time of a daily commute across the river, most of the textile factory workers now lived on the Sergipe side. There was new housing there to accommodate them.

What about the manufacturing sector here in Penedo? I remembered a big factory down in Bairro Vermelho. I asked Francisco what kind of factory it was. «*Sabão*» (soap), he said, «*mas acabou-se.*» *Acabou-se* in the case of the soap factory means 'washed-up'.

The *usinas*, where they process sugar and alcohol from cane, were now in their seasonal shutdown, casting their workers into unemployment.

Well, what else in the way of factories, then? Francisco slapped his fingers against one another and said, «*Nada*» ('nothing').

He explained that a very influential mayor, the one just before I came to live here in 1968, had set the policy for Penedo's economic development. That policy was not industry, but tourism.

That mayor didn't want industry, because he viewed it as inevitably polluting. Why, Coca-Cola had wanted to build a plant here in Penedo, but the mayor wouldn't let them. (I have never thought of Coca-Cola as polluting, except to those who drink it.)

So, today, Penedo is free of industry. But not of pollution; its residents produce plenty of that.

Francisco laid the blame on the municipal administration. The current mayor, he said, is a doctor who got elected on the basis of his good work in social welfare projects. But he has no organizational skills and is a drunk besides. That very night a meeting to initiate impeachment would be held.

One Penedo business that was booming was the

vehicle ferry service across the river. Francisco told me the same story about the bridge as had Adriano. The owner of the ferry service, I surmise, is a very wealthy man. By the nature of the operation, however, he employs a mere handful.

The ferries do generate some drop-off income at a few riverside gas stations, luncheonettes, and bars. Nonetheless, the trucks carried over by the ferries usually zip through town without stopping and most of the money in the pockets of the passengers on the buses and the drivers of cars passes through Penedo to be spent elsewhere.

As for retailing, the shopping area of Penedo is about six square blocks in the center of the old town. The stores sell mostly small-scale stuff—*miudezas*, domestic items, stationery, groceries, medicines.

Pharmacies are numerous and profitable, because nearly everybody is *doente* (sick) frequently. Many cannot afford, or don't trust, doctors, and so they self-medicate, trial-and-error, eventually spending more on medications than the doctor may have cost. What would be prescription drugs in the United States are available here over-the-counter. I myself resorted to self-medication to treat my intestinal affliction.

One entrepreneur has bought four stores in the area, and, under the group name Lojas Diana, sells a wide variety of items through them, in the manner of Walmart on a small scale. Francisco told me that the owner of Lojas Diana is trying to acquire a monopoly of retailing in Penedo. I wondered whether that was possible...or worthwhile.

Penedo does have one example of modern retailing it lacked in my time,—a warehouse-size supermarket.

What contributions the five banks in Penedo make to local economic development I cannot determine in my short time here, but the fact that none of them has a *câmbio* or cashes traveler's checks is evidence that their contribution to sustaining tourism, the purported town development policy, is nil.

What about that tourism? Penedo, another Olinda, another Ouro Preto! Penedo, the tourist town that tourism has never discovered. Let's assess the infra-structure for tourism:

For accommodations, Penedo has the Hotel São Francisco, which I have already described. EMBRATUR rates it three stars, but I think one of them is a random smudge of ink. The Pousada Colonial is attractive but small. There are a half-dozen other lodgings, more suitable to the scruffy student tripper than to the freespending tourist. One hotel is the Imperial, whose name, like that of the Magestic, is a grandiloquent falsehood; another is the Turista, mere wishful thinking.

Penedo has only three good restaurants, two of them in hotels, the other this one on the *Rocheira*. Were the many luncheonettes in town located in the United States, the local health department would send in storm troopers armed with fumigators.

On the positive side, the *Prefeitura* has staffed the great churches and historical buildings with friendly guides, like Rogério, Adriano, and my Gilmara of the Corrente. There is a hospitality being extended to tourists.

Also, more sites are open than in my time. But São Gonçalo and the Paço Imperial ('*Dom* Pedro II, the Emperor of Brazil, slept here') have been shut tight for a long time. Penedo is not Rome, where, if Santa Maria

Maggiore is closed for restoration, you've got 299 other churches to choose from. Penedo has so little, that what little it has should all be available.

The woeful city services I have already described, so I won't rehash the same trash here.

What is the biggest booming business in Penedo? Actually, I found the answer to that question on my very first morning here. It's the *feira*. The *feira* has grown in extent geometrically, while the rest of the economy has grown only arithmetically. And what is the *feira*? Farmers-in-the-market, the peasant economy of food and subsistence.

When I asked my informant to compare the economy of Penedo twenty-five years ago to today's, he said, *«Mesma coisa»* ('the same thing').

Francisco leaned on the rail and stared out over the river. As for today, he said, there's no employment, no revenues, no development.

If that's the case, I responded, what will be Penedo's future?

Francisco slapped his fingers together again, in a dismissive gesture, and said, *«Mesma coisa. Nada.»*

Thursday, April 6. Penedo.

. . . diarrhea and vomiting this morning, as my body wrote a strongly worded, critical restaurant review of Brazilian cuisine...

* * * * *

Confined to bed all day today. Severe headache, pain in my hip joints. Too weak to get out of bed and walk across the room for a drink of water.

At least the nausea, shakes, retching, and spurting quit.

Well, I've gotten down to the level of the locals, at last.

* * * * *

If I had to live in this place very long, I'd go nuts.

Wait a minute, what am I saying? I already have lived in this place very long,—two years.

There were nearly forty Peace Corps volunteers in Alagoas when I arrived in 1968. A year-and-a-half later, they were all gone...except me. I outlasted every single one of them, I the last Peace Corps volunteer to serve in Alagoas.

Well, then, hasn't my physical and mental toughness been proved? What's the problem?

I still say that if I had to live in this place very long, I'd go nuts!

Friday, April 7. Penedo.

I hired a taxi to take me on the grand tour of Penedo.

Like the other towns of any size in Brazil, Penedo has its *Centro* (in Penedo's case the riverfront and its first few streets inland) and its various *bairros*. *Bairros* are neighborhoods, not precisely delimited geographically. *Bairros* give residents a belonging between the family and the municipality.

Penedo has three principal *bairros*. In the lowlands upriver of the *Centro* is Bairro Vermelho. Another riverfront *bairro* is Bairro Oitero, downriver of the *Centro*. The uplands of the town is Bairro Duro. When I lived here, I used to tell people that I resided in Bairro Duro, although, in fact, I was out aways from the town on the rural road to Coruripe. My Peace Corps colleague Mark lived on Penedo's special landmark, the *Rocheira*.

I told the taxi driver about my earlier residence in Penedo and my return to visit. I could cover the *Centro* and the *Rocheira* on foot, already had, actually. I wanted him to take me on a circuit of the *bairros*.

I got in the taxi, and we bounced off over the *paralelopipidos* (the black paving blocks of the streets).

Most houses in Penedo front the street or sidewalk (if any). Only the well-to-do have a front yard. The houses are typically one level, three or four rooms, shutters rather than glass windows, the exterior of plaster painted in pastel colors, the roof of clay tiles out of the tradition of Mediterranean Latin housing. Most houses in Penedo have indoor plumbing, I think, the traditional *chafariz* now fallen into disuse.

Gilberto Freyre called Penedo the city of *sobrados* (multi-story residences), but, like much in Freyre's writing, that is exaggerated. The *sobrados* of Penedo are conspicuous but few and mostly concentrated in the *Centro*. A more typical dwelling is a modest rowhouse.

As far as quality of housing goes, Penedo does not have its good areas, bad areas. Side-by-side on any street you might see: A building of the last century, abandoned and dilapidated; next, a house newly plastered and brightly painted, with fresh flowers in the window; then, one that hasn't received any maintenance in a decade, but looks OK; next, a house whose roof, devoured by termites, has collapsed into it; then, behind a landscaped yard, a big, beautiful modern house with satellite TV dish on the roof, and so on.

The sequence of houses might be interrupted by a fenced yard with its pigs and chickens or an empty lot strewn with debris and garbage. Don't look for any consistent neighborhood character in Penedo.

The town has sprawled out over the surrounding area. Penedo now had 68,000 people, the taxi driver told me.

There were various housing developments, conceived and constructed as discreet communities. Even though originally built as what we would call low-income public housing, some of these seemed more thriving than the town itself.

We passed a ceramics factory. The mud of the bank of the Rio São Francisco is still put to utilitarian purposes. The various clay jugs and bowls in my house on the *sítio* used to make me feel like a citizen of the ancient Roman Empire. Clay is cheap and serviceable; just don't drop it. I remember visiting the ceramics workshops across the river in Carrapicho. The workers spun the lumps of clay on a wheel set in motion by pumping a foot-pedal.

Judging by all the plastic pails and bowls I saw in the *feira*, I think clay has been superseded by plastic, although, if the plastic wastebaskets of the Hotel São Francisco are representative, the plastic is cheap and prone to crack. Unlike potsherds, plastic pieces do not reintegrate into the bed of the river.

Some parts of Bairro Duro appeared prosperous. Perhaps optimism, individual initiative, and entrepreneurialism have moved to the periphery of Penedo.

What I especially wanted to do on my taxi tour was to find my old house on my *sítio*. The young woman in the stationery store told me that my *sítio* had been subdivided for housing. That information would forestall any disappointment I might feel at what I would find.

We drove around Bairro Duro looking for the road to my house. The *chafariz* that was the local landmark no longer existed, the young woman in the stationery store had also told me. Perhaps all the houses near my *sítio* now had piped-in water.

My driver wasn't sure where to go, but some locals set us on the correct course.

We found the triangle where the *chafariz* had been. Yes, that was it; I remembered the layout of the triangle. So, off to one side must be the *sítio* of *seu* Manoel, my landlord. Still there, but untended. Well, then, my house should be a few minutes down the road along the other side of the triangle.

We drove down the road, my eyes looking for my

house. I saw one that might be it. Its position and orientation were right, but it seemed bigger than my house as I remembered it.

We drove along farther. We came across an intersection, from which the road began a descent. No, I lived on the up-and-up, not on the decline. My house must have been the one we saw.

We reversed our course and stopped at the house. It was in poor shape. A front porch had been added, the side veranda expanded, but it was my house all right.

The owner was within. Hailing him and explaining my interest, I asked his permission to visit. He unlocked the gate. He lived behind, not the palisade of sticks I knew, but a white wall topped by barbed wire.

By studying the number and arrangement of windows and doors, I was convinced that I had found my house.

Out back I came across the privy and shower—the shower the very same concrete cabinet I had had to cleanse my virile young body.

My house, my *sítio*, home at last!

What joy and satisfaction I felt to be there, even for those few minutes. I took some photos to make permanent what my senses would experience but briefly.

The *sítio* itself was, indeed, gone, its area cut through by brick walls, between which small houses had been erected. These new people were not cultivators, for the number and variety of fruitbearing trees were much reduced. Nonetheless, the taxi driver prevailed upon the householder to give him a bag of mangoes.

Just down the road, a wealthy doctor had built himself a grand estate, with high walls all around, the house itself an imposing pyramid. A pharaonic fantasy on a dirt road leading out of Penedo.

For the rest of it, the road I once lived on was worse. There were more houses and more people; such crowding has caused wear-and-tear, a degradation of the landscape. Much of the tropical beauty was gone.

I thanked the householder for indulging me. *«Uma boa morada aqui»* ('A great living out here'), he said. Yes, but he didn't know the half-of-it. The house may have been the same, but, with the setting destroyed, the *morada* was not the same.

The taxi driver and I completed our circuit by going through Bairro Vermelho. Some mud-and-wattle hovels down there. At least it doesn't flood in Bairro Vermelho anymore; Paulo Afonso has seen to that. And they still could plant some paddy rice, the driver told me.

My tour ended on an unpleasantry.

Before getting into the taxi, I had told the driver exactly where I wanted to go and how long I expected the tour to take. I asked him three times how much he would charge for such a tour; but he gave me no answer. Don't worry, he said, he was an old-timer known by everyone, and would be fair with me.

In my own mind, I thought fifteen *reais* would be a good charge for such a tour. If I had to pay more, I might just ride the buses around town and try to find my *sítio* on foot.

When the tour ended and I asked him how much I owed, the driver said thirty *reais*. I protested. Immediately, it became twenty. I didn't want to spoil the mellowness of my mood of nostalgia by a protracted haggle after-the-fact, so I gave him the twenty. All over the world, it seems, taxi drivers deserve their reputation.

Well, never mind that. I had found my house on the *sítio* at last. It's somewhat the worse for wear but persisting. Not very different from myself.

* * * * *

I had found it difficult to recognize my house, because of remodeling changes made by its current occupant, but there was one constant in its furnishings, that is, the hammock on the veranda.

The hammock is a fitting symbol of tropical lassitude. The first time I climbed into one, at that moment, I began going native. The hammock is indeed native. The aboriginal Indians of Brazil used to sleep in hammocks. The invading Europeans brought their beds with them, but, when they discovered that the organic stuffing of the mattresses was susceptible to infestation by local vermin, the Europeans imitated the Indians and took to sleeping in hammocks.

The hammock is very space-efficient. For the poor of the *nordeste*, who live in one room, an immobile bed would take up too much of the interior living space. Lifting one end of the hammock from its hook and hanging it on the other hook on the back wall opens up the bedroom for use as parlor and dining room. Sleep may be put aside, making way for wakefulness.

We commonly associate death with sleep, the coffin

with the bed. In the *nordeste*, a deceased whose family is too poor to buy a wood coffin is carried to his grave in the hammock he had slept away his life in.

So, the last use of the hammock; but there is a lifetime of good napping and sleeping to be enjoyed first. Lying comfortably in a hammock takes a little art, however. You have to lie on a diagonal, if you don't want to wake up from nap or sleep with a terrible backache.

My colleague Mark used to sleep in his hammock, but I myself could not get used to an entire night in one. I like to sleep on my stomach or on my side; the hammock was always bending me the wrong way. Before I took up residence on my *sítio*, I bought a bed frame. Aware of the problem of insect infestation, I had a piece of inert foam cut into mattress size; Maria Heléna's mother sewed a cover for it. And so I slept away my nights according to European tradition.

I was native Brazilian during the daytime. Every day after lunch, I used to take a book and resort to my hammock on the veranda of my house. The book proved an alien intrusion of the intellectual into the sensual. Under the drowsy spell of the midday heat and the shushing of the rustling palm fronds, I would doze. My hand would go limp and the book fall to the floor of the veranda.

What happened to the book once happened to me. I almost became a casualty of the hammock. One of the hooks, the one attached to the window frame, must not have been properly tempered steel, for, little by little, it was straightening out, without my noticing it. One day, as I dozed, the loop at the end of the hammock slipped over the hook and, unsupported at one end, my body plunged to the concrete floor of the veranda. My bones were rattled, I was shaken from my slumber. After circumambulating the *sítio* to determine that my skeletal and nervous systems were intact, I returned to the veranda, hammered down the hook, and climbed back into the hammock.

The worst injury done to me during my Peace Corps stay in Penedo was when, one night, a sneak-thief crept into my *sítio* and stole my hammock from the veranda. I immediately went out and bought another one, which I kept safe inside at night, under my bed, where I could guard it.

When I found myself taking to the hammock before lunch or even directly after breakfast, I had to admit to myself that I was succumbing to the inertia of the *vida tropical.*

The Portuguese word for hammock is *rede* (HED-jee), which means net, like a fishnet. Some hammocks are such a net-work of cordage, squares of open space being left between warp and woof. It would seem that an open mesh would be cool, but I do not like that kind of hammock. The openings admit insects to the attack, and the cordage is rough on bare skin. Also, the transverse poles at each end turn the hammock into a tense pallet.

The best Brazilian hammocks, those from the *nordeste* state of Ceará, are made of tightly woven cotton, dyed in bright colors and patterns and decorated with tassels along their fringes. They wrap up around the body like a comforting cocoon.

The motto sewn on one hammock I owned was *Dorma Bem, Viva Feliz,* ('Sleep Well, Live Happy.') You can live happy in a hammock without necessarily sleeping, for a hammock may be shared. Besides the single-width, called *solteiro*, meaning 'bachelor', there is a double-wide, called *casal* ('couple').

Sharing a hammock is a test of compatibility, as any *nordestino* will tell you. I myself passed the test once, failed it once.

There was a long and languid afternoon on a *sítio* owned by Maria Heléna's family, where I attained intimate hammock compatibility. Maria Heléna and I, side by side but becoming one, pulled the edges of the hammock around us, wrapped ourselves in each other, and experienced tropical ecstasy.

On another occasion, in Recife, with someone else, every move I made displaced her, every adjustment she made discomforted me. And so on, a whole sleepless night, all attempts at accommodation futile. But then she too was an American, the two of us awkward strangers in a native Brazilian *casal* hammock.

So, not every sharing of a hammock is enjoyable.

Alone, anyway, suspended, you seem to return to the primordial security of floating in the amnion in the womb.

You might have been visualizing swinging in a hammock, but there should be very little motion, really. A hammock is not a playground swing or a trapeze. Twist your pelvis just slightly to set up a little motion, or, if your hammock is near the floor (where it should be for safety, as I discovered), push off from the floor with your hand. Some attach a cord to the wall, drape it over the hammock, and tug the cord gently if they want motion. But again, you want to be afloat, not tempest tossed.

When I returned to the United States from my Peace

Corps service, I brought a new Ceará hammock with me. (It was a *solteiro*, not a *casal.* I must have anticipated a reversion to temperate-zone human relatedness.) I had some hooks too. Yet, I never unpacked the hammock and set it up. A hammock in Chicago? The Brazilian artifact was as out of place there as, after two years in the tropics, I was to find that I too had become.

* * * * *

Besides pangs and sighs, a nostalgia trip should yield up a little laugh now and then. I got one when I stepped into the restaurant of the Hotel São Francisco for lunch.

Some of the tables had been arranged into a square U, in front of which was a stand with flags. On the head table was a bell topped by the cogwheel of commerce, and, at its side, a gavel. A Rotary Club luncheon.

When I was a Peace Corps volunteer, the Penedo Rotary Club found out I was living in town and invited me to address their gathering. Then, as today, their weekly luncheons were held in the Hotel São Francisco.

On my Peace Corps subsistence allowance, I couldn't afford meals in the restaurant of the Hotel São Francisco. Now I would be given a free lunch, in return for a little palaver. I ate heartily, then rose to address the Rotarians in my best prandial Portuguese. I informed them of the Peace Corps and its activities in Brazil and in Alagoas, and of my own ventures in Penedo. My presentation filled the time when they were using their toothpicks.

The president of the Club saluted me on my fine work, and I returned the compliment to the Rotary—

(although I had no idea what they did and wished one of them would attend a Peace Corps luncheon to tell us about the activities of the Rotary).

Everybody duly saluted and complimented, we all went our separate ways, to *descanso* and digestion.

During my two years in Penedo, I never had any collaboration or, indeed, any further contact, with the Rotary. Was I just a curiosity, to be given a one-time exhibition? Had my presentation been deficient in entertainment value? Shouldn't we all be in community development together?

Further along in my autobiography, I would be hooked up with the Union League Club Foundation of Chicago, another backslapping, good-eating, society of fraternity and philanthropy. I endured many of their smug luncheons.

We can't choose those we work with, but I hope to retain that right regarding those I dine with. And I hate the business lunch. I can't bow my head in the grace prayer, follow the agenda, pay attention, ask and answer questions, propose or second motions, applaud an honoree, receive a plaque myself, eat, drink, and take the napkin to my beard, all at the same time.

Anyway, in search of more information on today's Penedo, I hung around in the bar, until the Rotary meeting concluded. When the Rotarians emerged, I collared one of them, who, by chance or by my good instinct, turned out to be the current president of the Club. What was the Penedo Rotary up to these days?, I asked *seu* Abílio.

They had only twenty members, he told me, so they couldn't conduct any grand programs. They dispensed pens and other school supplies to needy children and toiletries and bread to the poorest of Bairro Vermelho. Mostly, they met to discuss the problems they had observed the previous week and then agitated authorities toward solutions. They even induced the governor of Alagoas to attend one of their meetings and listen to their concerns, an earful to accompany the bellyful.

Abílio repeated the refrain on the ineptitude of the municipal administration. And he was pessimistic on the economy—national, regional, and local.

Well, I shouldn't mock the Penedo Rotarians. They do what they can with what they have. Any group voice is louder than the cry of an individual.

In a small town, you can find some connection with nearly anybody, if you talk with a person long enough. It turned out that Abílio was a student in the English class of *dona* Lorinete, one of the schoolteachers I used to teach English to every week. So, Abílio is my grandson, linguistically speaking. However, in our conversation we spoke not one word of English.

Abílio asked me how long I would be in town. A certain eagerness in his eyes made me suspect that he would invite me to address the next luncheon.

It's not necessary for me to relive every single experience on this nostalgia trip. I told Abílio that, unfortunately, by the time of their next meeting, I'd be gone from Penedo, gone from Brazil.

* * * * *

Oh no, not *the bridge* again.

Abílio told me that there was a plan to build a new bridge to link up the coastal interstate highway being laid down for the tourists.

But will it be built here at Penedo or downstream at Coruripe? Abílio and the Rotary Club have petitioned the governor and lobbied on behalf of Penedo.

'If we don't get the bridge,' Abílio lamented, 'all the traffic will pass by upriver and downriver. Penedo will become a deserted island.'

The bridge! *Mesma coisa.* Same old thing.

* * * * *

I spent a few hours with Padre Aldo, a priest I had known through my Peace Corps role. In that role I had obtained a USAID grant for the construction and operation of a pre-school health center, the oversight of which would be by Padre Aldo.

First we sat in the lobby of the Hotel São Francisco and interviewed each other on what has transpired this past quarter-century.

Padre Aldo has been a priest for forty years. He is paunched, stooped, and feeble. He has not been well, but he still has that cackling laugh of his. He is a great talker and mixer.

After some general discussion about Penedo and mutual acquaintances, I narrowed down the topic to the situation of the Church in Penedo.

Padre Aldo told me that the bishop, in his dotage, had retired, so Penedo was without a bishop. As for ecclesiastical staffing, Penedo, a town of 45,000 people, he said, had only two priests, one of them a German octogenarian; there was also one religious brother.

Padre Aldo himself divided his time between Penedo and Arapiraca, the latter town more dynamic in religious life, as in other aspects of comparison. But Padre Aldo was *penedense.* He couldn't sever his ties with his hometown. So he had adopted a shuttle-ministry.

I wondered whether Padre Aldo would be the last priest produced by Penedo. The *crentes* have infiltrated the religious void.

Padre Aldo invited me into his car and directed the driver to take us on a tour. He showed me some rowhouses that had been built for the poor by the diocese.

We stopped at Lar de Nazaré, an orphanage founded by Padre Aldo more than thirty years ago. I never expected an orphanage on the itinerary of my nostalgia trip—(I have no nostalgia for my own five years in an orphanage)—, but there I was.

Built as an orphanage and trade school for two hundred children, the Lar de Nazaré now housed fifty boys and girls, eight to eighteen years old. The building was deteriorating, parts of a ceiling had collapsed, walls were crumbling. There was litter everywhere, little cleanliness within.

There were separate wings for boys and girls. The dormitories were old-time institutional, the beds in close rows all together in a huge room. There were little pink plastic dolls on the beds of the girls.

Padre Aldo took me through refectory, bakery,

kitchen, classrooms, printing shop, woodshop, auditorium, playground.

In the playground, one boy complained to Padre Aldo that another boy had struck him, and showed his swollen eye as proof of his allegation. Another boy was sitting on a low wall, head-in-arms, crying. The boys were just milling around randomly. A youth worker was there, but he seemed only present, not involved.

The girls, by contrast, sat side by side on the benches. They smiled sweetly as we greeted them. They asked Padre Aldo for his blessing, and he gave it to them. When they pressed him for individual blessings, he answered, 'I bless you all. There, now, you're blessed enough.'

Padre Aldo introduced me to a woman on the staff. When she found out I had been a Peace Corps volunteer, she mentioned a pen-pal exchange she had participated in as a student of *dona* Lorinete. Another part of my past recaptured. I was the one who had arranged the pen-pal letters between a Penedo class and one in Wisconsin. Lorinete, Maria Celina, and I had translated the letters. The woman told me that she still had the photo of her pen pal.

We left the Lar de Nazaré and made a stop at the *Inspetoria*, the administrative offices of the local schools. When the teachers found out about my one-time connection to their work, they made a big fuss over me. They complimented me on my Portuguese. I said just enough not to force them to correct their first impressions of the competence of my usage.

Much of what was to be seen on my tour was little different had Padre Aldo taken me on the same itinerary in 1968. The phrase, *Penedo, a mesma coisa*, keeps recurring during every local foray I venture upon.

Outwardly, Padre Aldo has little to show for his forty years of priesthood in Penedo. What is it that one man with meager resources can do? I admire Padre Aldo's vocational loyalty and tenacity.

* * * * *

This afternoon, the goal of my nostalgia trip was accomplished.

A nostalgia trip is a risky undertaking, I warn you about that. You may go back, but you won't like everything you find. And there is an inclination to psychological unwholesomeness in any return to the past. The writer, a reflective, and, so, retrospective type, is especially prone to unwholesome nostalgia. *Saudades* are not peculiarly Brazilian.

You can go back, but you cannot live it again. Why go back, then? Not to see which buildings are in ruins and find out which acquaintances are dead. Loss is the unwholesome part of it all. Yet, there is something in your past life, which, if revisited, may have a salutary effect on your current and future living.

The course of our lives is random and disjointed. It lacks a coherence that would imbue it with meaning. Much of what we live through we don't really experience deeply, until much later; it takes a long time for our lives to sink in. A nostalgia trip, belated assimilation, can provoke an understanding of significances.

At lunch, I had felt a bit uneasy in the head. What was it? Yesterday's affliction lingering? Some new infection asserting itself? Culture shock, maybe?

After lunch, I took to bed.

After my *descanso*, I felt better as I toured with Padre Aldo.

My traveler's checks nonnegotiable, I needed some local cash. Aline, a desk clerk, told me that the woman who operated the hotel's boutique was going to the States, to Disney World; she would buy the two fifty-dollar bills I had secreted in my belt.

The woman wasn't in, so I sat around in the boutique waiting for her. And that is how the accomplishment of the goal of my trip came about.

The most important aspect of life in a small town like Penedo is sitting around and talking to people. If you don't know them, you will get to know them. And they will tell you important information, including just what you wanted to know but had no idea whom to approach to ask.

Two ladies, both longtime employees of the Hotel São Francisco, happened to be in the area where I was waiting. I told them about myself and my ties to Penedo.

In this community, you only need to engage in conversation with a couple of people, in order to tap into the lines of personal relations that connect everyone here.

One lady knew *seu* Manoel, the now deceased owner of my *sítio*. She led me up the street to meet his daughter, *dona* Cleonice, whom, of course, I once knew. *Dona* Cleonice had transformed the old printshop into a senior citizens' ladies' club, which was now in full session.

When I was introduced to *dona* Cleonice, she let out a scream of stupefied delight and threw her arms around me. She marveled at my miraculous reappearance and laughed and reminisced. She told me how highly her father had thought of me,—I never failed a rent payment—, and she updated me on her children, whom I had known as teenagers.

I had walked by the building before but had not recognized it. Today I found something more important than the building. I found the living people within.

The lady from the hotel and I returned to the boutique to sit around and wait for the one who would buy my dollars.

Nearby was the elderly lady who operated the newsstand. When she heard me mention the Hotel Magestic, she said that she knew its family intimately. She began to tell me about them all. I asked questions about each, especially about Maria Heléna. The lady answered my questions, and I found out.

She referred to Maria Heléna by the affectionate diminutive of her name and described her, as I myself remembered Maria Heléna, as *«tão delicada, tão carinhosa»* ('so genteel, so affectionate'). And wasn't I Maria Heléna's *namorado*?, the lady asked. I nodded.

Some of what I heard about the various members of the family of the Magestic was sad, some heartening. There is no escaping that bittersweet combination in the fates of human beings.

I will not tell you here all that the elderly lady told me, for it is more of personal private significance than general interest. But, for me, what I heard fulfilled my deepest longings and motivation for my trip. I had made contact, even if only in words, once again.

I found out what I had wanted to know, from two people I had just met, in a situation where I was trying to accomplish something else, something much less important.

Yes, I felt some pangs in my heart, deep disturbing emotions, the pain of memory and loss. The accomplishment of a return is something of an ordeal. But, in all, I felt a wonderful satisfaction.

Penedo and its people, ever dear to my heart! The two years I lived here were a tiny fraction of my life, but of what significance to me, as I have realized only so much later.

I love you, Penedo, I love your people, I love my memories of you.

A nostalgia trip is not a return to a place. It is a return to friendship...and to love.

Saturday, April 8. Penedo.

A teenage girl in the municipal tourism office told me that she desperately wants to learn English. She is enrolled in a special language school, which she attends two hours per week. I tried to get across to her that two hours per week did not show sincere desperation.

She wrote some words on a piece of paper and asked me what they meant. W-a-t-e-r, she thought, meant *mesa* (table). What about l-e-t-t-e-r? I explained to her that it could mean one of two things—a letter you mail to somebody or a letter of the alphabet.

As she was writing the English words and asking me about them, I was apprehensive that she would write some obscenity someone had maliciously taught her; if so, I would give the word a random innocent meaning.

She told me that some American from New Jersey had visited Penedo twice and gone out with her. Maybe that was what accounted for her desperation to learn English.

Her grasp of English, from what I could decipher of the words she wrote down—(she too timid to even attempt to pronounce them)—, was a hodgepodge of misunderstandings.

What were they teaching her in that school, anyway? (Keep in mind that her teacher is probably a *penedense* who set himself up as an English teacher. Methinks there are no native English speakers now resident in Penedo, except myself, for ten days only.)

Well, before she can walk through the door of the school, she told me, she must say, "May I come in?" If she doesn't, or if she says it incorrectly, the teacher refuses to let her in. Once, she just had a mental block, she said. Couldn't even remember the "May" part. Before she broke into tears, however, the teacher relented, told her the phrase, and admitted her.

What kind of methodology was that, imposing an obstacle upon the willing student? As we say in English, "Katy, bar the door!"

What about the content of the instruction? She told me that the teacher would give them sentences in Portuguese to translate into English. OK, model sentences. I as a Berlitz teacher have used model sentences (but directly in English). One model sentence she had been given was:

«Aquele ferreiro é o meu inimigo.», which she translated correctly as: 'That blacksmith is my enemy.'

What kind of model sentence is that? The teacher should be teaching useful everyday phrases, and upbeat material at that. Her teacher should have given her this model sentence:

«Aquele ferreiro é o meu amigo.» ('That blacksmith is my friend.')

Yes, that's what language learning is all about, making new friends. God knows, a blacksmith, obsolete, unemployed and with no prospects of future employment, could use a friend these days.

The girl invited me to drop in on her class tomorrow evening. How everybody, the teacher included, would be delighted to speak English with an American, she said.

I didn't think that would be such a good idea. You know how, at some moments, your mind just goes blank and you can't think of some common word or phrase? What if, after my three weeks of total immersion in Portuguese here in Brazil, I stood on the threshold, faced the eager students, and just couldn't come up with the "May I come in?" Or, worse, what if the teacher dragged me into his anti-blacksmith campaign? No, I won't get drawn into that. I never met a blacksmith I didn't like. (Well, all right, I have never met a blacksmith, but I abhor on general principle the language of prejudice and group hostility. If I ever do meet a blacksmith, I want to have a good word for him. W-a-t-e-r, for example. He'd probably like some after all those hot, sweaty hours at the forge.)

Rogério happened to be in the building, with Adélebra. Rogério and I spoke in Portuguese, until Adélebra drifted off to talk to someone, whereupon Rogério jumped to take advantage of my presence to augment his eleven years of English learning. He asked me, "How many long time you are marry?"

After a few more sentences of that stuff, I reverted to Portuguese. Let Rogério put up with my solecisms and barbarisms in his language—(that was a requirement of hospitality)—, not the other way around. Enough of linguistic wanderlust. This is Brazil. Let's speak Portuguese!

The young people of Penedo are desperate to learn English. So am I. I've put in many more than two hours per week, but I haven't really learned it yet. A writer is trying to learn his own language by teaching himself. I hope I have a more competent teacher than does the girl in the Penedo tourism department.

If she ever manages to get to New *Joisy*, I told her, then she'll really learn some words. Meantime, she should get serious about her study of English. I myself always am. How many long time I am studying it!

* * * * *

I stopped in to see my last unvisited major architectural landmark of Penedo, the Teatro Sete de Setembro. (The name on the building spells the first word *Theatro*, which is not correct Portuguese spelling. Like our own *theatre*, a foreign affectation, a deplorable abuse of language.)

That local cultural institution was operated by no less august a body than the 'Imperial Philharmonic Society, Seventh of September.' The designation *Imperial* was bestowed upon it by the Emperor of Brazil, *Dom* Pedro II. The Seventh of September alludes to the date in 1822 when his father, *Dom* Pedro I, had declared the independence of Brazil from Portugal.

'Independence or Death!', *Dom* Pedro cried out. (American independence was launched with a Declaration, Brazilian with a Shout.) No deaths proved necessary in the revolution, because *Dom* Pedro was of the Portuguese royal family. The Brazilian Revolution turned out to be just a division of family property.

Inaugurated in 1884, the theater was the first one in Alagoas. That's not saying much, I admit, but any cultural initiative brings renown to a town.

I read on a plaque that the restoration of the theater was financed by the Banco do Brasil. I've said so many disparaging words about the Banco do Brasil, but let me here give it recognition for doing something constructive.

——Which reminds me. While I was in Maceió, I attended a film, a slapstick colonial epic called *Carlota*

Joaquina.

The king of Portugal, *Dom* João VI, and his wife Carlota had escaped the armies of Napoleon by fleeing to Brazil. Carlota was a woman of nymphomaniacal drive; she proceeded upon a carnal itinerary of the male bodies of the colony. Carlota had arrived in Brazil with race prejudice, but, discovering a black stud who pleased her, she converted to Brazilian miscegenating promiscuity.

Her long-suffering husband dealt with Carlota's many lovers in a humane, but effective, way. He would award them some lofty title and position, then ship them away to their new duties. In the scene in the movie that drew the biggest laugh, *Dom* João said to the black man (who, on his knees, trembled in fear that he might lose his head for cuckolding the king), 'For your many and great services to the Crown, I appoint you: President of the Banco do Brasil!'——

The work financed by the bank was more a reconstruction than an authentic restoration. The original fabric of the building was probably too decayed to permit reuse of its materials.

Anyway, it's a fine theater, an oval with three tiers of balconies around its perimeter. The Teatro Sete de Setembro seats six hundred people and accommodates another hundred standing. It lacks the gold and the Baroque embellishments of the Opera House of Manaus, but is otherwise comparable. People come to see the show, not the building, after all.

My young guide gave me an excellent private tour of the entire building—seating areas, stage, dressing rooms, costume and set-design rooms, and noble salon. I did have to slow him down, as he rattled off dates and statistics, so that I could translate them into digits in my head.

I remarked to the guide that a theater is less interesting as an empty building than as the setting for a live performance of some kind. Were performances being held in the Teatro Sete de Setembro?

'No,' he said. 'People here stay home and watch TV. They don't put much value on culture.'

That seemed like a harsh judgment.

I remembered that, during our long conversation in the Pousada Colonial, Eric described *penedenses* as *«uma gente culta»* ('a people of culture'). A moment later, he reconsidered, saying that, anyway, they used to be—a long time ago.

That accorded with my own recollections. When I lived here, Penedo was the only town in Alagoas that was cultured. A certain class of people in Penedo was ravenous for culture. They would plead with me to teach them English, to tell them about the United States and other countries I had been to, to discuss music and art and ideas.

To me, culture was taken for granted. Hey, I had grown up in Chicago. Even gotten a university education in Europe. Culture was popcorn.

Those *penedenses* who so hungered for culture have since either given up and lapsed into the commonality or moved away to Recife or some other place that gratifies cultural appetite. Penedo has become a deserted island in more ways than in the traffic pattern of the country.

The Imperial Philharmonic Society, Seventh of September, is long gone. The Teatro Sete de Setembro is an empty building. It is open, you can enter, but you will not hear the sounds of culture within.

* * * * *

If there is a competent handyman in this country, I've never seen him at work, nor have I found any proof of his existence.

All of the various mechanical apparatuses in Brazil, it seems, were either incorrectly installed or never given proper maintenance. So they fail, are *fixed*, and then fail again.

Even what works in Brazil doesn't work quite right. You learn to appreciate the approximation of functioning.

If only I had my toolbox here with me, I'd get my own hotel room, at least, in working order. I'm not a mechanical wizard; my education was more academic than technical. Still, compared to the maintenance crews I see around me, I'm a regular Handy Andy.

I'm not talking sophisticated stuff here. Just the sticking door, the drawer in the armoire with the sagging bottom that impedes opening of the drawer below it, the dripping faucet—that kind of thing.

As for cleaning, I see people working away at it, but nothing is clean. Sanitary ineptitude everywhere.

There should be an international law that countries may not advance to higher forms of technology until they prove competence in the lower ones. The World Techno-judge would say, "So, Brazil, you want a nuclear particle accelerator, eh? All right, first show me how you clean the filter in that air-conditioner."

Speaking of which:

After nearly a week of me hauling and dumping the pailfuls of water dripped from my air-conditioner, the hotel finally sent in a repairman. He hooked up the hose to the drainhole, using some kind of putty.

I was skeptical about the repair. Sure enough, as I look out onto the balcony now, I see that the air-conditioner is dripping, not neatly from one hole as before, but in various places along the seam in the bottom of its case. Now I'll have to get some more pails to deal with the new problem.

* * * * *

I have to wonder whether the image of rampant crime and violence in Rio de Janeiro and São Paulo is a gross exaggeration, a free-floating anxiety induced by the sensationalistic media.

There is a Brazilian TV program called *«Aqui/Agora»* ('Here-and-Now'). Patterned after the American real-life dramas, it includes segment after segment of police chases.

In Brazil, with the *polícia militar*, a police operation is more like a commando attack. A platoon charges forward, machine guns drawn, as a helicopter hovers overhead. As we have found out from recent reports, the Brazilian police would just as soon shoot the suspect as arrest him.

While the chase is going on, the TV reporter breathlessly pursues the pursuing police, stopping only briefly to shove the microphone into the face of a distraught relative of the victim.

Such vivid imagery creates a stronger impression than any printed tables of actual crime statistics. I remember a peaceful Rio, a congenial Rio. Has it really changed into the Detroit or Newark of Brazil?

A waiter in the restaurant on the *Rocheira* told me that he is a *penedense* whose family had moved to Rio. On three separate occasions there, he had been the victim of strong-arm robbery, the knife in his ribs or the revolver in his face. Each time, they took his wallet and watch. He didn't have much for them to steal, really. Nonetheless, three times he suffered the suspense of possible violent death-at-that-moment.

Finally, he resolved to come back to Penedo. You couldn't earn much money here, he said, but living was more important than making a living. He was glad to be back in Penedo, where he felt safe.

'Is there much crime in Penedo?' I asked the driver who took me on the taxi tour.

'Oh, no,' he answered, as if I had asked a nonsense question. 'The people here are religious, peaceful.'

Rio de Janeiro may have been turned into a combat zone, but Penedo persists as a haven of peace-and-quiet. That is one aspect of the *mesma coisa* that is heartening.

Regarding law-and-order, Penedo is Mayberry.

* * * * *

On Saturday mornings, Penedo bustles with the

feira. By Saturday midafternoon, however, the vendors and buyers have all dispersed, either on trucks or horse-drawn carts down the roads or on the boats up or down the river.

The stores close down. Avenida Floriano Peixoto then looks like the main street of a ghost town. Except for an occasional solitary sweeper or a stray dog drifting through, the town seems evacuated.

At dusk, the cantina of the Hotel São Francisco opens. I descended to have a beer at one of its sidewalk tables. The waiter, hearing the scratch of my chair across the pavement, emerged from the inside. There was no one else in sight. The casanova of the sidewalk bar had not yet arrived to set up his stalking station.

Just after dark, a steady flow of people, mostly teenagers and young adults, began appearing from a sidestreet and walked past my table. Where were all those people coming from?, I asked the waiter. Mass in the cathedral had just let out, he explained; they were now going to spend Saturday evening socializing in the *praça* by the riverside promenade.

One young couple didn't make it that far. They separated from the flow and crossed the street into that little park where I had observed the man watering the shrub.

There was a low white wall there. The young man sat upon it, spread his legs, and pulled his *namorada* to him. The rest of the crowd coming from Mass passed them by.

There were a few preliminary words between the couple. Then, kisses and caresses, strokes and fondlings, with cool-down pauses now and then. At last, they pressed together and began to rock into each other against the wall.

Distracted by them, I poured the beer up my nose, choked, and snorted foam onto the table.

That performance-in-the-park, casual as it was, proved more provocative to a mere onlooker than any cinematic pornography.

First having paid conventional service to Christian love-thy-neighbor, the young lovers were now at their true devotion, to each other, a carnal liturgy after the spiritual one.

I wished myself there in his place, as in Penedo days of long ago. How could I not succumb to such a bit of nostalgic fantasy?

Just a few moments of that, however. I'm here as a sociologist, not as a voyeur; and, necessarily, an outsider, no longer a participant.

I dried my whiskers on my sleeve, paid for my beer, and withdrew myself from the disturbing over-stimulation.

I wondered whether Murilo and Eric were down at the Pousada Colonial. I needed to restore my instinctual calm by a protracted discussion of the agricultural economy....

Sunday, April 9. Penedo.

Very early this morning, I took a stroll to the *Rocheira* to enjoy the panorama of dawn over the river.

There were earlier risers than I. In the river below, I saw a dozen narrow boats floating in the stream. The fishermen were already in quest of their catch. Their jokes and singing wafted up to me, where I stood perched on the high rock.

In the trees on the cliffside, I saw hummingbirds (in Portuguese, *beija-flores*, 'flower-kissers') flit and dart among the branches.

On the *Rocheira*, there is an ancient cactus, its trunk turned to treelike bark, but its green upper stems still bearing flowers and fruit. I watched a small bird tearing out straws of an old nest in the cactus. He plucked them, then flew off to his own nest somewhere, an excellent conservationist, recycling building materials.

Penedo has its natural life of river and land and air, but I have not paid them much notice thus far. People and their activities so dominate the scene, that it is easy to forget that there is Nature here, too.

To observe Nature in Penedo, you must look in the off-hours—for the birds of the dawn or the bats at dusk. And your itineraries must be conducted in the outplaces—small neglected overgrown lots wedged between buildings, or on the islands of the river, or at the periphery of town. This is Brazil, the Tropics. Even so, except for the weather, Nature is not so conspicuous as you might think. Most of the birds in Penedo are caged ones. And every plant and animal you see belongs to someone.

The *penedenses* expect the river to yield up, day after day, the fish to feed them. Eric told me that commercial fishing is no longer feasible in the Rio São Francisco. Yet, as I saw in the *feira*, there are plenty of fish to be had.

From my belvedere on the *Rocheira*, I looked down upon a fisherman paddling himself back upstream. His basket was open; it had not been filled, but I could see a layer of slim silvery fish in its bottom. He and his family will have a good Sunday dinner tonight.

The *penedenses* take their river for granted. Most of the pollution so far, I think, has been organic, rather than industrial, so the fish survive. The dams have caused a disruption, certainly, but maybe that has been only a redistribution of the fecundity of the waters to the impounded lakes upriver.

The Rio São Francisco at Penedo has entered a chronic low-water state. There is nothing the *penedenses* can do about that; they have no say in federal development projects. In the future, Penedo will have less river, more mud.

Near my hotel, I noticed a building with a sign that said, *Clube de Pesca de Penedo* ('The Fishing Club of Penedo'). I've been here a whole week and have yet to see a window or door of that building open. I suppose they forgot to post that other sign on the door, *'Gone Fishing'*.

* * * * *

On this, my last day in Penedo, I wanted to ascend to the roof of the Hotel São Francisco to take photographs, then hire a sailboat for a cruise of the river.

Nature gave no consideration to my wishes, for She frustrated both my intentions by sending in the deluges.

As the rains started, the birds, instead of seeking shelter, launched themselves into the air. Rising up to the descending waters, they bathed themselves in an aerial shower, and, with a mid-air twitch and shake, drained off the dusty water from the tips of their wings.

I heard a sound familiar to me from the old days, but which I hadn't heard these previous dry weeks—a chorus of frogs. Frogs, suddenly, as if by spontaneous generation.

In Brazil, if you have the American attitude of "I'm going to do it right now," you won't last long. No, if there is something you want, you've got to lay the groundwork, make the personal contacts, ingratiate and fenagle, interpret refusal as tentative, persist good-naturedly, wait, be frustrated but not take it seriously, then, at the opportune moment, make your move and achieve your objective.

That's what I did in the matter of the rooftop photography from the Hotel São Francisco. First, I tried the direct approach. I made a surreptitious ascent of the steps on my own, to see whether I could accomplish my goal without involving anyone else. But I found the exit door to the roof padlocked.

I then tried a bottom-up approach in the hierarchy of the hotel. I asked the friendly chambermaid to help me get onto the roof for my photography. No problem, she said. She'd get the key from the maintenance man right away. But she returned shaking her head. Only *senhor* Andrade, the hotel manager, had the key to the roof.

Well, then, I would have to take the roof door problem to the top. I had already engaged the hotel manager in several conversations and solicited his approval to get a small cash advance off my credit card. He would be accommodating to my request, I thought.

But it was the weekend, and *senhor* Andrade made only brief stop-offs at the hotel. I found out from the saucy Aline when he would be arriving. Last night, it was after dark, no good for my purposes. This morning, Aline said, he would come in after 9:30, but, by then, the rains had arrived too.

Senhor Andrade is a harried man, with an anxious look, always running around in a sweat, herky-jerky in his motions, breathless in his speech. He is the wrong type for this environment. With the condition the hotel is in, *senhor* Andrade has a lot to worry about.

Even though it was raining, I went down to the front desk to make my request. Oh, *senhor* Andrade shrugged, he had given the keys to some handyman, who had not returned them. Maybe tomorrow, he said.

'But I'll be leaving for Recife tonight,' I pleaded.

In that case, maybe *senhor* Andrade had another set of the keys.

He went into his office, then emerged with a look of satisfaction and a ring of keys. He handed them to Aline, to hold for the eventuality of a respite from the rains.

An hour later, seeing daylight, I ran for the elevator to go down and get the keys from Aline, before the next wave of rains arrived.

From the sixth floor, I ascended the stairs to the roof. Behind the locked door I found another locked door, but the ring had the keys to both. I wondered why there had to be such high security for an otherwise inaccessible rooftop. Had distraught lovers recently jumped to their shared suicide from the rooftop of the Hotel São Francisco? Had some cat burglar gained access from the roof? Or had the hotel employees merely been up to some mischief up there, removed from their boss's surveillance?

Anyway, I gained access, the rains kept their distance, and I was able to shoot my aerial panoramas of Penedo and the Rio São Francisco valley.

On the roof, I could see what a neglected state the physical structure of the hotel had fallen into; but, then, I already knew that, from inside information.

The key to effective living in Brazil is *jeito*. You've got to have *jeito*, or, if you don't, then you've got to induce someone who has *jeito* to use his on your behalf.

Jeito is the ability to get what you want or to get something done, a know-how peculiarly Brazilian. *Jeito* is not necessarily knowledge or training or even high position, though those may help. The one with *jeito* is like the spider, with his fingertips on all the strands in the social web. A lot of *jeito* is in whom you know; that's why random socializing is so important.

Ter jeito means to have *jeito* yourself. I did live in Brazil two years, I speak Portuguese, I know Penedo, so, speaking about myself, I can say, *«Eu tenho jeito.»* ('I've got *jeito*.') I did succeed in getting access to the rooftop.

However, regarding my other goal for the day—my sailboat excursion against the obstacle of the weather—

well, that was a matter for disposition, not by Brazilians, but by heaven, where, unfortunately, *Eu não tenho jeito.* Still, on Sundays, heaven sometimes grants favors even to atheists.

Seeing a gap in the waves of storms, I thought I'd venture my attempt. Today is my last day here, my last chance.

Walking down the *Rocheira* and descending to the landing in Bairro Vermelho, I looked about for a sailboat to hire.

The first one I saw was a beautifully painted craft, with a sail fore and another aft. Its name was *Jerusalem.* It was long enough for a dozen passengers. Would it be worth the owner's while to take me out solo? If so, how much would it cost?

The old pilot was snoozing on the deck. I called to him and inquired about the hire. He sent a boy to fetch the owner. But the owner, it turned out, had just left town. I wouldn't be able to hire the boat without the owner's approval. Alas, I never entered *Jerusalem.*

There was one other boat moored nearby, smaller than the first, but also with two sails. The advertising on the sails was for Coca-Cola. Things went better with Coke.

The owner was fetched, and we agreed to a charge. The owner's name was *seu* João.

I would describe *seu* João as a "wizened old salt," but he has spent his sailing life on fresh water. Anyway, the two adjectives apply.

When he was eighteen years old, he told me, he

descended the Rio São Francisco from Pão de Açucar, a dryland town up in the *sertão* of Alagoas. He stayed in Penedo and took up sailing, which he has done for a half-century now, for *seu* João has turned seventy. He has an amiable disposition, like most *penedenses*, and one good tooth.

It took us a few minutes to realize it, but *seu* João and I had seen each other before. The night I had discussed economics with Francisco in the *Rocheira* restaurant, there was only one other person there, seated at a table, an old man whose only impression on me was his big flopping ears, for he sat at the other end of the restaurant and had his back to me. That was *seu* João.

He and Francisco were great friends, he said. Whenever he took people on excursions, *seu* João would suggest dinner at the *Rocheira* restaurant afterwards. Likewise, when a customer at the restaurant asked what there was to do in town, Francisco would recommend a sailboat *passeio* with *seu* João. It was a mutually advantageous friendship the two of them had.

Anyway, the night of my dinner at the *Rocheira*, Francisco had related to *seu* João the story of my past in Penedo. *Seu* João was going to approach me about a *passeio* on the river, but I paid the bill and left while he was distracted by a conversation with the cook. Now I had found him, so it had all worked out.

With the assistance of a young man with a few more teeth than *seu* João, we cast off. The first few minutes of our cruise were slow, because the *Rocheira* blocked the winds, but, as soon as we were clear of it, the sails filled and we began a swift course downstream.

How beautiful Penedo looked from a distance!

Seu João's boat was in the same aged condition as he was, but she floated. The mate bailed out the water from the rains earlier in the day. I asked *seu* João how long his boat was. Sixty palms, he said; he didn't know how long that was in meters.

We swung around an island and headed downwind, upstream.

I asked *seu* João whether he received money for advertising Coca-Cola on his sails. No, he said, all he received was the printed sailcloth. I informed him that *jangadeiros* in Maceió received 700 *reais* every six months for their advertising. *Seu* João's empty jaw dropped. He then said that he had heard that, in Aracajú too, the sailboat owners received cash to advertise. Now informed of the realities of the market, *seu* João looked determined to renegotiate his contract with Coca-Cola.

We approached Carrapicho, on the Sergipe side of the river. *Seu* João asked me whether I'd like to put in for a visit. 'Why not?', I answered.

The boys of Carrapicho were sprinting their horses along the shore. One boy had his horse in the river, where he was giving it a good washing. Maybe he thought clean horses ran faster.

I went ashore and walked around a bit. Not much there. Like Penedo and the other riverside towns, Carrapicho developed uphill, so I'd have to do some climbing if I wanted to check out the town.

There were pottery artisans there, but, it being Sunday, I didn't think they'd be at work. If they were and I entered a shop, I'd be expected to buy something. With all the baggage and *lembranças* I already had, the last thing I needed was a big clay pot to load on the back of the donkey.

What decided me was the look of the sky to the seaward side. More storms coming. I directed *seu* João to cast off.

I asked him about the pottery manufacture of Carrapicho. Wasn't it being put out of business by plastics? They sold most of their production to the poor towns of the *sertão, seu* João answered, but, even so, he thought their pottery expensive. They also made some finely finished wares for the tourists. Indeed, I had seen a display of Carrapicho ceramics at the ferry landing in Penedo, but there were no customers milling around the display. Another local industry gone to pot.

As we rounded the big island of São Pedro, the deluge arrived. I sprung open my little white umbrella, which I had the foresight to bring along, and which Janet had had the earlier foreforesight to purchase and outfit me with before my departure from the States.

We battled wind and rain, me huddling under the umbrella, *seu* João throwing an old canvas around his bony shoulders, the mate just letting himself be watered.

Suddenly, from a flat sandy island, a man waved his shirt, hollered, then jumped into the river. With flailing arms and grasped shirt held high, he swam toward us, battling current, rain, and the waves whipped up by the wind. Like the two boys I saw last Sunday, he was a reckless venturer upon dangerous waters.

I lost sight of him as he approached the boat, but soon his knuckles appeared over the bow, and, little by little, advanced toward the stern. The mate helped him with an awkward entry over the gunnel. *Seu* João scolded him for coming aboard on the windward, rather than the leeward, side.

The man had been on a picnic with friends on the island, but the rains drove the picnic spirit out of him. Besides, he explained, they still had a lot of undrunk beer on the island; he wanted to be able to get up for work tomorrow morning. (It was only 4:00 in the afternoon.) Exercising sober self-discipline, he had leapt to his own deliverance.

The squall now having passed inland, I retracted my umbrella.

Getting a good look at me, our hitchhiker presumed that I didn't know Portuguese and began to inquire about me to the other two. I told him I knew Portuguese, so he could address me directly.

I related some of my life story, and he commented upon it. He thought Chicago was in California. Even after I explained the geography to him, he kept saying, 'Chicago in California.' He called Chicago, *o Capital do Frio* ('the Capital of the Cold'). He was right, at least, about that, and in more ways than he knew.

We sailed past the old soap factory, so I inquired further about it. It was shut down fifteen or more years ago, our dripping newcomer told me. No one in Penedo had the resources to put the building to any other use, even though it would make a splendid market, capacious warehouse, or new factory to provide employment to *penedenses*.

The building was an imposing bulk. There had been some salvaging of its materials, but not much, considering the passage of time.

Our new passenger told me that he himself had salvaged 4,800 clay roof tiles from the site. He had sold them off, lot by lot. Now, it turned out, he was building a new house for his family, but he had no tiles for its roof.

Why didn't he buy tiles with the money he got from selling the old tiles?, I asked him.

That money was already gone—«*aqui*»; and he patted his bare belly.

The four of us then exchanged jokes and jests about the man once rich in roof tiles, now with not a single one to cover his house, and about tiling roofs with money, and about laying away a few tiles for a rainy day, and so on.

Our talk then got around to the most important one present—The Rio São Francisco. Our passenger rattled off the names of the impounding dams that have been built on it: As Tres Marias, Sobradinho, Paulo Afonso, Xingó. He intoned the names several times, ominously, as if calling felons to the dock. That's what they were, really, because they were stealing the water from the lower São Francisco.

There was a good side to it, he admitted. He remembered that, in the days before the river had been fully subdued by the dams, 1979 he thought it was, the São Francisco had inundated the lower bairros of Penedo. Fish swam in the streets. But was that worse than drying up the river? He referred to the river by the local nickname, *Velho Chico*, something like our *ole man river.*

Seu João remarked that soon the river will be *calado*. The word means "quiet"; the imperative of its verb means "Shut up!"

I don't know whether I should attribute elegiac sentiments to the old sailor, but it seemed to me that *seu* João meant that the speech, the flow, of the river would be silenced. That's the way I took his remark, anyway.

How could my return to Penedo have been complete without that *passeio* in a sailboat, without seeing Penedo from the perspective that many of the locals have? The river is not of Penedo; Penedo is of the river.

We put in, and the four of us bid farewells. *Seu* João said that, upon my return, he would be pleased to take me out again, if he were still alive.

I doubt that I will ever come back to Penedo, having finally and fully assimilated its significance to me. Nonetheless, even if *seu* João does not live to see tomorrow's dawn, his type will live on, as long as the Rio São Francisco does.

Return

Monday, April 10. In transit, Penedo to Recife.

On every leg of my trip, I have arrived in a place without seeing how I got there. Or, at least, I have taken a dark view of things along the way.

This time I deliberately kept myself in the dark.

In planning my return from Penedo, I had hoped there was a remnant of air service, or that, by inquiring about the comings and goings of guests at the Hotel São Francisco, I might hitch a plane ride back to Recife. Idle hope, that, for Penedo's air links have vanished into *acabou-se.*

Brazil has no interstate rail that covers the entire country, so I would have to get to Recife by bus. But what kind of bus?

I remember the *carro leito*, the deluxe express bus service of the old days. Many medium-sized cities unserved by air or the airfares too expensive, little rail to speak of, fewer people owning cars, the *carro leito* had been developed to carry long-distance passengers in style. The buses were the most modern, air-conditioned, and equipped with toilets and plush seats, which were assigned. (No, I don't mean that the toilets were equipped with plush seats or assigned; I mean the general seating was like that.)

My Peace Corps subsistence allowance didn't permit regular use of the *carro leito*, but, once, I did scrimp for a ride on one. Even in the pitch-and-roll of the puddled highways in the rainy season, the *carro leito* was a dream.

I seem to remember a stewardess aboard. She provided pillows, served drinks, and played hostess. (My memory may deceive me on that point, for, in my youth, I used to suffer stewardess fantasies.)

On this trip, when I spoke the words *carro leito* to the bus company clerks in Maceió and Penedo, they looked at me as if I were still suffering fantasies. No, there was no more air-conditioned, express *carro leito* service in the *nordeste. Acabou-se* again.

I could take the Alagoas line back to Maceió and there transfer to another company's bus to Recife. There was a 6:00 A.M. bus from Penedo to Maceió. If I did that, however, I would have to haul my baggage around the terminal in Maceió, wait there an hour or two for the connection, be in doubt about seat availability, and take the trip under the hot sun in a bus without air conditioning. On the other hand, I would be able to see the sights along the way.

My one alternative was direct service to Recife, of which there was one bus per day, or, rather, per night, leaving at 9:00 P.M, three hours after sunset this southern hemisphere autumn season of the year. The pro of that choice was no hassle and uncertainty in Maceió; the con was travel by night once again.

I decided to go directly to Recife.

When it came time to check out of the Hotel São Francisco, they had no record of my prepayment of the daily rate, despite the fact that I had made the arrangements two months before arrival and had had them confirmed, first in Rio, then in Maceió just a week-and-a-half ago.

The charge items on my account were written in

pencil; the clerk tallied them with a hand calculator. He then put the statement into a manual typewriter and hunted-and-pecked away.

Wise to the likelihood of unforeseen delays, I had allowed plenty of time to get to my bus, but, even so, the hitch at check-out pushed into the leeway. I gave the clerk the phone numbers of the Brazilian agencies involved with my trip and told him to confirm my prepayment with them. I then paid the incidental expenses and hurried out the door.

This time I had engaged the doorman to help me carry my bags the ten blocks to the bus station. Fortunately, there was a respite in the rains.

As we walked down the hill, the doorman said to me, 'I don't think you'll be back in Penedo,' because, he said further, I seemed *«desanimado»* ('downhearted'). He was a perceptive psychologist.

I boarded the bus, but at 9:00, the scheduled departure time, I heard two bad sounds. First, the clink of a steel tool onto the paving blocks near the front of the bus. Second, the words *«Tem que trocar.»* ('We'll have to change it.')

Now, this was a bus that had sat riverside in Penedo all day, plenty of time for any repair. The half-hour before scheduled departure the driver had spent leaning against the wall romancing a young woman, except for the few minutes he was dipping into the bus fuse box, pulling fuses, examining them, and putting them back in place, as if trying to decide which piece in a box of chocolates he wanted to eat.

Now, at departure time, it was out-with-the-tools. We passengers, already boarded, sat immobile. A retarded boy circled the bus and waved goodbye to us, crying out in a distressing falsetto.

At last, the tire replaced, a half-hour late, the bus got into motion. We climbed the streets of Penedo toward our exit.

I immediately felt a pang of separation.

Bus service is necessarily slow in Brazil, due to two aspects of the manner-of-operation.

First, bus service is not terminal-to-terminal. Instead, you can ask the driver to drop you off at any intermediate point you want, and, if you know the usual route of a bus, you can flag it down and get on.

That seems more like urban transit than intercity operation, yet, in Brazil, it has its justification. There may be no public transportation to and from the terminal, no available or affordable taxi service, no friend with car to take you. So, the bus companies accommodate you as they can. That's good service to some, but a protracted agony of delay to those like me going from terminal to terminal.

More objectionable is the bus company's toleration of all the stuff that passengers load onto the buses. One wiry little man and his grinning adolescent accomplice loaded into our bus baggage compartment fourteen gross pieces: Four motors mounted on boards, five boxes reinforced with steel strapping, two frames something like stepladders, and three squares of junk lashed together. That was not passenger baggage; that was industrial freight.

Between the *pinga-pinga* (the 'drip-drop' of pickup and discharge of passengers) and the freight loading and unloading, a trip on a Brazilian bus usually takes a time disproportionate to distance. It would take us seven-and-a-half hours to go from Penedo to Recife, a distance of 250 miles.

We headed into the now black interior of the state of Alagoas. We made two major stops—at Arapiraca and at Palmeira dos Índios, the two towns that, I had been told, had surpassed Penedo in Alagoan importance. Even from what little I could see from the bus at night—in the way of commercial property, industrial enterprises, quality of housing, general extent and appearance—it was evident that both towns had indeed advanced. By contrast, Penedo seemed a hamlet sinking into the mud of the Rio São Francisco.

I had reserved a window seat for myself, not to continue my neverending quest for the *Cruzeiro do Sul,* but to insure myself some ventilation. I was frustrated in that design, however.

The windows on the bus were very wide. The passenger in the seat in front of me could open and close a window to his front and another to his side, the passenger behind me had an operable window at his side, but, as for me, I found myself stuck with two sliding panes of overlapping glass.

The man in front of me must have had some kind of new artificial hairpiece. Every few minutes, he would turn on the light over his head and examine his hair in a little round mirror.

His hairpiece was hideous, (but of course his friends will say, 'Nobody can tell it isn't real. You look great!'). I don't know what it was made of, but every time he combed his hair, I could hear it.

Because of his hairpiece, he didn't want any open windows near him. I could understand that. What if, with the bus speeding along in a sudden 60 mph burst, the piece flew off? Worse for me, what if, while I was half-dozing, the hairy clump flipped and plopped straight into my face? I would relive my longago nightmare of being attacked by a vampire bat.

Maybe he would get off at an intermediate stop, after which I could open the window and get some air. No, with my luck he'd go all the way to Recife. His hair was probably being recalled by the manufacturer.

I sneaked my fingers between the curtain and the pane and opened the window next to him, just a tad, enough to give me air but not so much as to derange his head.

All of a sudden, I thought I detected the odor of skunk. I didn't remember that Brazil had skunks, yet, Nature Norm of the North knew a skunk when he smelled one. Or was it the man's hair? No, because, when he detected the odor, he shut tight the window.

In a few minutes, I had reopened the window just a crack. Not satisfied with the flow, I reached for the handle again, only to feel the eerie touch of his fingers over mine, as he slid the window shut.

On into the interior of Pernambuco.

I awoke from my doze, when the bus stopped to pick up waiting passengers near Bom Conselho. At the front door of the bus, I saw a woman with a baby in her arms; the baby was bundled in a hooded sweater. Nearby, another woman stood with shawl covering her head and shoulders.

Had I slept away several nights, to find our wayward driver had gotten us lost in the Andes? No, this was Brazil still. These people were highlander Brazilians.

The Brazilians describe the climate of such interior Pernambucan towns as Bom Conselho or Garanhuns as cold. A Chicagoan, native of the *Capital do Frio*, would call it temperate and scoff at the lady for overdressing the baby.

It couldn't have been very cold, for I spotted some Giant Toads prowling about. Giant Toads are the biggest in the world. They emerge at night to feed, especially relishing some stray dog they can catch napping.

There were Giant Toads on my *sítio*. I discovered them by the thump-thump-thump outside my door one night. Thereafter, I never ventured out to the privy after dark without kerosene lantern and my machete.

The Brazilians call Garanhuns *'the Switzerland of Brazil'*. That analogy belongs to the same category of misrepresentation as the description of Recife as *'the Venice of Brazil'*. (I'd like to see some Brazilian travel agency promote Venice as *'the Recife of Italy'* and Lucerne as *'the Garanhuns of Switzerland'*.)

I had intended to take an excursion to either Garanhuns or Caruarú from Recife when I was staying in Olinda, but my bout of illness prevented me. Now I would see both of them, even if by night, coming back from Penedo. Intention realized, not in one way, but another. The going home is part of the trip, too.

I was surprised to see the streets of Garanhuns full of young people at this 1:00 A.M. of a Monday morning. I didn't know Garanhuns was such a party town. I noticed they were all coming from one direction; maybe they had attended a show or dance.

A woman got on the bus with a girl about nine years old. The woman was big boned and had the face of the Indian on the old buffalo nickel. Her hair was gray and pulled back. I think she was the girl's grandmother.

Back in Penedo, two hale-fellows-well-met had gotten on and taken the two seats across the aisle from me. Later, the one by the aisle moved off to get himself a window seat. The woman now occupied the vacant seat and put the girl on her lap, despite the facts that the girl was big and there were still vacant seats on the bus.

The old woman then began to cough. It was a tubercular cough, if ever I heard one. That scared the hell out of me, because I know that tuberculosis is my doom; it'll come back and get me sooner or later. And there on a bus with no air, in the dark of night in Brazil, an emissary of Tuberculosis had come to get me.

As her cough continued, the man in the window seat next to her also began to show concern, for, he, after all, was closest to, and trapped by, her.

Then the girl in the woman's lap threw up. Tall as she was, she puked onto the white seatcover in front of her and onto the shoulder of the sleeping passenger there.

The old lady took no notice or didn't care. But the man next to her now had a look of revulsion and panic on his face. He quickly squeezed past the old lady and the girl and retreated to the farthermost seat in the back of the bus. Now the girl and grandmother occupied side-by-side seats.

The one who had been thrown up upon awoke,

discovered the abuse he had suffered, cursed the girl, and fled down the aisle. A young woman in the window seat in front of the old lady and girl, suffering the aroma of the vomit, began to pull the seatcover off with two dainty fingers. She handed the seatcover to the old lady, who, uncomprehendingly, tried to give it back to her. 'Drop it on the floor,' the young woman told her.

The old lady continued to cough away. When will she get off this bus?, I asked myself in increasing desperation. Please, God, let it be just lung cancer, not tuberculosis, I prayed. Something noncommunicable.

I felt so fortunate in the seat mate I had acquired. He was coughless. He reeked of liquor, true, but he could keep it down. He snored so innocently, so harmlessly, by my side.

The old lady and the girl got off in Caruarú. While waiting for the driver to open the baggage compartment, the old lady pulled out a pack of cigarettes and puffed away between coughs.

Caruarú is an artisan town, renowned for its folk art, especially the painted clay figurines of peasant life. I had been unable to get there from Olinda, as I mentioned, but, in compensation, I bought a Lampião and Maria Bonita made in Caruarú.

What I now thought about on the bus, however, was the Passion play at nearby Nova Jerusalem. This being Monday of Holy Week, the Passion play was in nightly session. The crowds had to be tremendous. Even Fernando Henrique Cardoso, the current president of Brazil, showed up there a few nights ago. Just when things had seemingly calmed down on the bus, would we now be invaded by pilgrims returning to Recife from the performance?

I needn't have worried. It was 3:00 A.M. The miracle of tonight's Resurrection *espectáculo* had been accomplished long before. The overstimulated devout had already dispersed.

A woman got on the bus with a teenager, her daughter as I judged by physiognomic evidence. The daughter had her arm in a sling. Whoever had done it seems to have intended to inflict the utmost of pain, for, instead of supporting the arm with the whole cloth, the arm hung on a slender strand at the wrist.

My seat mate having gotten off, the woman sat down next to me, her daughter in the seat opposite, the one where the pulmonary and gastric horrors had occurred.

I was trying to sleep again, when I felt the woman tapping my shoulder. She wanted me to change seats, so that she could be next to her daughter. The poor thing shouldn't be left alone.

No, I wasn't going to get up in the dark bus lurching and pitching about, move to snuggle up with lingering tuberculosis bacilli, or stumble down the aisle in search of new seat mate trials. Anyway, the woman was already sitting next to her daughter across the aisle, wasn't she? What did she want to do, hold the girl's hand? If her hand was broken, the girl wouldn't want it held, anyway. I ignored the woman, turned on my side, and tried to sleep.

The rest of the bus trip, like this telling of it, dragged on and on. Over every hill I looked for Recife, but it wasn't there. We had been scheduled to arrive in the middle of the night. If all continued to go as it had, we'd arrive near dawn. ...

My taxi driver in Recife was a tough looking

character. Tired from the bus trip, I felt in a non-communicative mood. Even so, I didn't think I should ride all that way with the driver without a word. These were, after all, the waning hours of my opportunities for contacts with Brazilians.

I complained to my driver about T.I.P., the new bus and metro terminal in Recife. They had built it of such immense proportions—(and, of course, my bus pulled in at the most remote bay and there were neither carts nor porters)—that I had had to lug my baggage farther than in most airports.

The taxi driver chimed in with my complaints. Ten years behind schedule in the opening and wrongheaded from start to finish, the T.I.P. was no good for anyone, he said. Those bus passengers who arrived at night and wanted a nearby hotel to sleep in until their connection would find no hotel near the T.I.P. And, with the T.I.P. so far from town, it would cost them more than their bus fares, as well as a lot of wasted time, to take taxis into town to a distant hotel and back. The T.I.P. was far from anything, farther out than the airport even. Why, you could get out of the country easier than get out of Recife to take the bus to Caruarú. Taxi drivers hated the T.I.P. too, he added as an afterthought. They were stuck with long trips and empty cabs on the return.

Recife greeted me with rains on my dawn arrival and a full overcast through this, a day of rest before the flights back to the States and home.

Weather and mood suitable to transition, from disengagement to return.

Tuesday, April 11. In transit, return, Recife-Miami-Chicago.

The Brazilians want to go to Miami. Why? What is Florida, but a slightly cleaner Brazil?

I'm among a planeload of Brazilians on their way to Orlando, to Disney World. Disney World? Brazilians already live in Fantasyland.

* * * * *

Back home, at the Villa Westmont.

In the wee hours of the first night, dreaming, thinking I'm awake. I, the vagabond, am climbing the highlands of Brazil in the dark. Where am I? What culture am I in?

Janet is with me, but I don't know what language to speak to her, Portuguese or English. Which is the language of our communication? I whisper some beautiful words in Portuguese: *«Ternura»*. *«Carinho.»*

. . . And so my nostalgia trip ends. In exhaustion and a little delirium.

GAZETTEER

ACAPULCO — Definitely located in Mexico.

ALAGOAS — State in the *nordeste* region of Brazil. Penedo is located in Alagoas.

AMAZON — Great river system draining the upper third of the South American continent. Its source in Peru only 180 miles from the Pacific, fed by numerous tributaries, the Amazon flows 4,000 miles across the continent to the Atlantic. Along its margins is an immense tropical rainforest (i.e., jungle).

AMAZONAS — The state of Brazil that encompasses most of the Brazilian portion of Amazônia.

AMAZÔNIA — The Amazon region; a geographical term.

ARACAJÚ — Capital of the Brazilian state of Sergipe. (A nondescript town, I had heard, but, in an incident not reported in the text, a native of the town spent a half-hour trying to convince me that my life would not be complete until I had seen Aracajú.)

ARAPIRACA — Second largest city in Alagoas, after Maceió.

ASSISI — Town in Umbria, Italy, hometown of St. Francis and cult capital of the Franciscan order.

AVENIDA CONDE DA BOA VISTA — Main street, downtown Recife.

AVENIDA FLORIANO PEIXOTO — Penedo's main street, named after an early president of Brazil, who was from Alagoas.

BAIRRO DURO, BAIRRO OITERO, BAIRRO VERMELHO The three principal residential neighborhoods of Penedo; described in the text.

BARCELONA — Major coastal city in Catalonia, in eastern Spain.

BARRINGTON — Suburb of Chicago; has one of the highest per capita incomes in the United States.

BELÉM — Major city on the Brazilian coast, near the mouth of the Amazon; capital of the state of Pará.

With a muggy, oppressive environment, Belém fits the tropical stereotype perfectly.

BELO HORIZONTE — Capital of the Brazilian state of Minas Gerais.

BOA VIAGEM — Urban resort beach of Recife, lined with highrise hotels; the *nordeste* version of Copacabana.

BOM CONSELHO — Small town in the interior of Pernambuco, near the Alagoas border.

BRASÍLIA — Capital of Brazil; built in the middle of nowhere (state of Goiás) in the 1950s and 1960s to promote development of the interior.

BRAZIL (Port. BRASIL) — Fifth largest country in the world, comprising nearly half of the South American continent; also the fifth most populous. Discovered by Pedro Cabral in 1500. Colonized by the Portuguese, against incursions by the Dutch and French. The only Portuguese-speaking country in the hemisphere. Currently, Brazil consists of twenty-seven states and a federal district (Brasília). Brazil considers itself developing, but, by some standards of comparison, it is underdeveloped, i.e., poor.

BUENOS AIRES — In Argentina, not in Brazil.

CALCUTTA — The city to which no other city ever wants to be compared in any way.

CAMPANIA — The region of Italy where Naples is located. Benevento is in Campania too, San Bartolomeo near the border with Apulia. Foggia is a major city in Apulia.

CARRAPICHO — Small town in Sergipe, across the river from Penedo; its main economic activity is manufacturing ceramics.

CARUARÚ — Big town in the interior of Pernambuco; known for its folk art, especially clay figurines.

COPACABANA — World-famous urban resort beach of Rio de Janeiro, now crowded and dangerous.

CORURIPE — Alagoas town, in the south of the state, near the Atlantic coast.

COSTA DOURADA — Literally, Gold Coast; a joint beach development project of the states of Alagoas and Pernambuco.
CRANE LAKE — Town in Minnesota providing access to the western end of the Boundary Waters Canoe Area Wilderness; described in *Nature Norm's North Woods.*
CRUZEIRO DO SUL — The Southern Cross, principal star constellation of the southern hemisphere.

DAYTONA BEACH — The Maceió of Florida.
DRAPER STREET — My "street of early sorrows".

EL DORADO — The mythical city of gold in Latin lore; metaphor for greed.
ELY - Town in Minnesota, gateway to the Boundary Waters Canoe Area Wilderness.
ESPÍRITO SANTO — State of Brazil, south of Bahia.

GARANHUNS — Big town in the interior of Pernambuco, with a supposedly Alpine climate.

ILHÉUS — City in Bahia, famous as the setting for Jorge Amado's novel, *Gabriela, Clove, and Cinnamon.*

JOÃO PESSOA — Capital of the *nordeste* state of Paraíba.
JORDAN (THE) — Baptismal river.
JUNQUEIRO — Town in the interior of Alagoas, between Maceió and Penedo; Rodolfo the *jangadeiro's* hometown.

LAGO DE JANAUARIO — A pond off the Rio Negro, a tourist attraction due to its *Victoria regia* water lilies.

MACEIÓ — Capital of the state of Alagoas; like many Brazilian state capitals, located on the Atlantic coast. Known for its beaches and coqueiros.
MANAUS — The principal city and capital of Amazonas.

Located on the banks of the Rio Negro, just upstream from its confluence with the Rio Solimões. Manaus is 1,000 miles upriver from the mouth of the Amazon.

MAUI — The "valley isle" of the Hawaiian chain.

MAXWELL STREET — Flea market area in Chicago.

MAYBERRY — Mythical TV community where the forces of law and order have nothing to do but hang around the barbershop all day.

MONTEVIDEO — Capital of Uruguay.

MUNDAÚ — A big lagoon in Maceió; it is connected to another lagoon, the Lagoa Manguaba.

NEÓPOLIS — Town in Sergipe, across the Rio São Francisco and downriver of Penedo.

NORDESTE — The Northeast region of Brazil. It includes the states of Bahia, Sergipe, Alagoas, Pernambuco, Paraíba, Rio Grande do Norte, Ceará, Piauí, and Maranhão. The *nordeste* is historically important, culturally interesting, and economically prostrate. Its economy is subsistence tropical agriculture devastated by recurrent drought in the *sertão*. Densely populated, but, in times of drought, subject to heavy out-migration to the *favelas* of the South-east.

NOVA JERUSALEM — Town in the interior of Pernambuco, setting for an annual Easter-week Passion Play.

OAKBROOK — Wealthy suburb and shopping mall west of Chicago.

OLINDA — Old colonial capital, in Pernambuco, just north of Recife. Known for its Baroque churches and artisans' colony. (Its name means "Oh, lovely!")

OURO PRETO — Hill town in Minas Gerais, south of Belo Horizonte. A Baroque showplace, one of the great culture sites of Brazil.

PAJUÇARA — Urban beach in Maceió.

PALMEIRA DOS ÍNDIOS — Town in the interior of Alagoas.

PÃO DE AÇUCAR — Literally, Sugar Loaf. A town in the interior of Alagoas, on the Rio São Francisco, but otherwise dry and hot-as-hell.

PAULO AFONSO — The main hydroelectric dam on the Rio São Francisco, managed from the town of the same name in Bahia.

PARAÍBA — State of the *nordeste*; borders Pernambuco on the north.

PASSAGEM — Ferry landing on the Sergipe side of the Rio São Francisco, opposite Penedo.

PENEDO — River town in southern Alagoas. Known as the capital of the lower Rio São Francisco; *o nosso querido Penedo.* Once the most important town in Alagoas, at least culturally, now in suspended animation or decline. I lived in Penedo as a Peace Corps volunteer from 1968 to 1970.

PIAÇABUÇÚ — Town in Alagoas, on the Rio São Francisco downriver of Penedo.

PIAUÍ — State of the *nordeste*, poor like the rest of them.

PONTAL DA BARRA — A little port in Maceió providing boat access to the lagoons.

PRAÇA BARÃO DE PENEDO — Principal public square in Penedo, site of both the *Prefeitura* and the cathedral.

PROPRIÁ — Sergipe's biggest town on the Rio São Francisco; it is far upriver of Penedo.

QUETICO — Provincial park in western Ontario. A northwoods wilderness area I discovered just after leaving Brazil in 1970. I have been canoeing it ever since, and, as Nature Norm, I've led group excursions there.

RECIFE — Capital of Pernambuco; the metropolis of the *nordeste.*

RIO DE JANEIRO — The old capital of Brazil. Once the most beautiful and congenial city in the world, now a mess of poverty, pollution, and urban pathology.

RIO NEGRO — A principal tributary of the Amazon; its name means Black River, describing its tint.

RIO SÃO FRANCISCO — A major river of Brazil. Originating in Minas Gerais, it flows northeast 1,800 miles to the Atlantic. Its lower section forms the boundary between the states of Alagoas and Sergipe. The Rio São Francisco is mostly navigable, but its natural flow has been altered by hydroelectric dams and impoundments.

RIO SOLIMÕES — A major tributary of the Amazon. It converges with the Rio Negro just east of Manaus at the so-called Meeting of the Waters.

ROCHEIRA — A huge, high rock outcrop overlooking the Rio São Francisco; likely the first point-of-settlement for the community of Penedo.

SALVADOR — Capital of the Brazilian state of Bahia.

SANTARÉM — City on the Amazon River, in the state of Pará.

SÃO PAULO — The megalopolis of South America, with some dozen million people. São Paulo (city and its state) is the economic powerhouse of Brazil. I've never been there—(it was described to me as the Chicago of Brazil)—and I intend never to go.

SÃO PEDRO — An island in the Rio São Francisco at Penedo.

SERGIPE — The state south of Alagoas; Brazil's smallest state.

SERTÃO — The arid interior of the states of the *nordeste*; afflicted by recurrent drought.

SOUTHEAST — The region of Brazil predominant in agriculture, industry, and commerce. It includes the states of São Paulo, Minas Gerais, Rio de Janeiro, and Espírito Santo, and Brazil's two biggest cities, São Paulo and Rio de Janeiro.

SURINAME — Ex-Dutch Guiana, small coastal country bordering Brazil. Its capital, Paramaribo, is a tropical stereotype.

TIVOLI — Suburb of Rome, site of the Villa d'Este, an extravagance of fountains.

VITÓRIA — Capital of the Brazilian state of Espírito Santo.

VOLTA REDONDA — Major steel mill near Rio de Janeiro, built after World War II.

WOODFIELD MALL — Mega-mall (250 stores) located in Schaumburg, a suburb of Chicago.

XINGÓ — A recently completed hydroelectric dam on the Rio São Francisco.

YORKTOWN — Shopping mall in Lombard, a suburb of Chicago.

GLOSSARY

(all words Portuguese, except where indicated otherwise)

abraço — warm embrace, the common greeting among Brazilians
acabou-se — all gone, done for, finished
a capella (It.) — singing without any instrumental accompaniment
agora (Gr.) — marketplace in an ancient Greek town (not to be confused with Port. *agora,* now)
Alagoano — a person from the Brazilian state of Alagoas
analfabeto — unlettered, illiterate
aqui — here

bairro — neighborhood
barraca — an open, roofed structure serving as a restaurant/bar
beija-flor — hummingbird
bichos — bugs, "little buggers"
boa — good
Bom dia! — Good morning!, Good day!
bon mot (Fr.) — witticism
Brasil Holandês — the seventeenth-century Dutch attempt to wrest Brazil away from Portugal

caboclo — originally, a person of mixed Indian-European race; now, a rustic, a hillbilly
caipirinha — a mixed alcoholic drink, made with *cachaça* (a crude rum), fruit juice, sugar, and ice
calado — quiet, still, silent
câmbio — international currency exchange
capitão — captain, (not necessarily the correct title of the crew chief of the *Amazon Clipper*)
carinho — love, affection
carinhosa — affectionate, loving, kind
carioca — a person from Rio de Janeiro
carnaval — Christian pre-Lenten orgiastics

carne — meat
carro leito — deluxe intercity bus service
casal — married couple; hammock-for-two
castagna (do Para) — Brazil nut
cebola — onion; also, descriptive name of a species of jellyfish
centavo — cent, one hundred to the *real*
Centro — downtown
chafariz — public spigot or fountain, for washing, a drink, or a source of water for those poor whose houses lack plumbing
cheio de — full of
cidade histórica — historical district of a town or city
Cisne Branco — white swan, the name of a schooner
coqueiro — coconut palm tree. Alagoas is reputed to have the most *coqueiros* in all Brazil.
crente — literally, a believer; refers to Protestants (as if Catholics are not believers)
culta — cultured

delicada — genteel, feminine
desanimado — discouraged, depressed, disheartened
descanso — nap, *siesta* (Why not explain a Portuguese word with a Spanish one?)
destino — destination; also, destiny
direto — express (more or less)
doce — literally, a sweet, and so it is. A gelatinous mass, fruit flavored, cut in slices from a tin; a cheap dessert
doente — sick
dona — a term of respect to a (usually older) woman, used with her first name; the feminine counterpart of *seu*
dona da casa — lady of the house

EMBRATUR — the Brazilian national tourism-promotion agency

EMPETUR — the tourism-promotion agency for the state of Pernambuco
espaço cultural — culture center
espectáculo — spectacle
Estrela d'Alva — Dawn Star, the name of a *jangada*
evangelion (Gr.) — the gospel

favela — the sprawling shantytown slums of Brazilian cities, now numbering more than 3,000
favelada (fem.)/*favelado* (masc.) — a resident of a *favela*
feio — ugly
feira — open-air market, held on the same day or days each week
fraco — weak, poor
frio — cold

gente — people, folks
gioco d'acque (It.) — a sudden turning up of the volume of fountains to spray or splash the unsuspecting, a Roman prank and favorite pastime of several eighteenth-century popes (the same psychology as the little boy with the squirt gun)
guaraná — popular Brazilian soft drink, once made from an Amazonian berry, now artificial flavor. (Guaraná used to be considered a potion and tonic; now it's just soda pop.)

igarapé — shallow-water openings in the flooded Amazonian rainforest, navigable by canoe
ilha — island

jacaré — alligator; otherwise cayman
jangada — the characteristic sailboat of the *nordeste*
jangadeiro — owner/operator of a *jangada*
jeito — the knack for getting things done, despite all obstacles; a necessary social skill in Brazil
Jívaro — an Indian people of Ecuador, known for their technological achievements in headshrinking

lago — lake
lagoa — lagoon
Lampião — a criminal who led a gang that terrorized the *sertão* of the *nordeste* during the 1920s and 1930s; despite his degeneracy and indiscriminate sadism, Lampião was turned into a folk hero. Gunned down by the *polícia militar* in 1938; as proof of death, his head was still on exhibit in Salvador in the late 1960s.
lembrança — souvenir
linda — lovely

machismo — the Latin delusion of the superiority of the male
mandioca — manioc, a starchy tuber, source of the flour that is a staple of the poor Brazilian's diet
Maria Bonita — gun moll of Lampião, Bonnie to his Clyde, gunned down with him in the big shootout with the *polícia militar.*
mas — but
matar — to kill; but, in certain idiomatic usages, to quench, satisfy, extinguish
mesma coisa — the same thing, same old thing
miudezas — odds and ends, notions
moçinhas — girly-girls
morada — living, lifestyle, way-of-life
mulatta (fem.)/ *mulatto* (masc.) — person of mixed, mostly African, race
museu — museum

nada — nothing
namorada (fem.)/ *namorado* (masc.) — sweetheart, lover
não — no, not
nordeste — northeast region of Brazil
nordestinos — people of the *nordeste*
nove — nine

paraíso — paradise (not on my itinerary)

paralelopipidos — parallelopiped paving blocks (a good Portuguese word for your vocabulary, if only for its rhythmic euphony)
passeando — strolling
passeio — walk-about-town, a daily ritual; also, excursion
paulista — a person from São Paulo
peixe-gato — catfish. (The manatee is *peixe-boi,* cowfish.)
penedense — resident of Penedo
péon (Sp.) — peasant
peristylum (Lat.) — an interior courtyard garden, rectangular, surrounded by a shaded colonnade; the architectural prototype of the cloister
piada portuguêsa — literally, Portuguese joke, the Brazilian version of the Polish joke
picolé — Popsicle
pinga-pinga — literally, drip-drip, bus service that makes many stops
piorou — it got worse
piranha — toothy fish of the Amazon and other Brazilian waters; not the devil as portrayed in lore, just a fish, really.
piscina — pool
polícia militar — the Brazilian police force
pôr-do-sol — sunset
pousada — inn, lodging
praça — a public square, a characteristic feature of Latin American, as well as of Mediterranean city culture; compare *piazza* (It.), *plaza* (Sp.), *place* (Fr.); a lot of socializing goes on in the *praças* of Brazil.
precisar — to need
Prefeitura — Town Hall, City Hall (both as building and administration)

querido — dear, beloved

real (pl., *reais*) — the unit of Brazilian currency, worth about $1.10 at the time of my trip

rede — net, snare, hammock (the snare of initiative)
rio — river; (if capitalized and used alone, the word means Rio de Janeiro)
rua — street; (*Rua do Sol* is Sun Street.)

sabão — soap
salvador — savior (if capitalized, refers to the capital of the state of Bahia)
samba — Brazilian dance, African in origin, the dance of *carnaval*
satori (Jap.) — insight, sudden awakening (a Zen experience)
saudades — a deep yearning for absent family, friends, or lover, or for places left behind; the word includes our ideas of homesickness, nostalgia, and romantic reminiscence, as well as our verb *to miss* someone or someplace.
schistosomiasis (a medical term) — a dread chronic disease contracted through immersion in contaminated fresh water
selva — jungle
sertão — the arid interior region of the states of the *nordeste,* frequently afflicted by drought
sete — seven (or nine or eleven or thirteen, as puzzled out in my story)
seu — contraction of *senhor,* a title of respect to a (usually older) man, used with his first name; compare *dona*
sítio — literally, site; a *sítio* is a house-in-the-country, surrounded by vegetation or an orchard on a few acres; the tropical version of a Mediterranean villa
sobrado — a home of several stories, a rare type in the *nordeste*
solteiro — single, bachelor; hammock-for-one
sombrero (Sp.) — literally, shade-hat (Mexican)
sujo — dirty

tão — so

teatro — theater
ter jeito — to have the ability to get what you want
ternura — tenderness
tolerância — tolerance, indulgence, leeway
trompe l'oiel (Fr.) — illusionistic art
tucunaré — peacock bass, a sought-after game fish, also edible

*uirapurú, (*Lat., *Leucolepis modulator)* — musician-wren, a rare singer who sings rarely
usina — processing plant for sugarcane, where they produce sugar and alcohol; long the principal industry of the *nordeste*

vagabundo — vagabond (In current Brazilian usage, the word denotes a good-for-nothing bum; in applying *vagabundo* to myself, I retain its classical meaning).
Victoria regia (Lat.) — royal water lily, largest in the world, diameter of pad up to six feet.
vida tropical — life-in-the-tropics, with or without ecstasy

~~~ END ~~~
~~~

About the Author

Norman Weeks is an experiential writer. He writes about living in Nature and within a culture.

Of the former, *Nature Norm's North Woods* relates his experiences in the woods-and-waters of the northland, while *Tropical Ecstasy* explores the Amazon and the Northeast of Brazil.

Of culture, he enters into one of the oldest civilizations in *Two Weeks in Eternal Egypt.* Culture-versus-Nature is a principal theme of *Walden* Contemporaneous.

The trilogy *Roman Ruminations* presents "the psychology of the human as an enculturated animal". Its three volumes are: *Loneliness*, *Instinct*, and *Love.* *Matters of Life and Death* contains further explorations into human psychology.

Some themes of *Symphony of Stories* are in the context of art, music, literature, and our contemporary technoculture.

Throughout his various writings, Norman Weeks expresses a cosmopolitan appreciation of our world and the wide range of experiences possible in one human life.

All these titles are available at amazon.com as Kindle eBooks, some also as paperbacks.

Made in the USA
Columbia, SC
22 November 2021

49263568R00154